FAITH OF OUR FATHERS

OTHER BOOKS BY JARVIS L. COLLIER

FAITH OF OUR FATHERS:
SPIRITUAL LEGACIES

Jarvis L. Collier

TownsendPress
Nashville, Tennessee

Dr. Lloyd C. and Lady Tressie Blue
Arlington, Texas
Gifted spiritual father, blessed wife, and family—
I applaud your contributions to the kingdom of God.

CONTENTS

ACKNOWLEDGMENTS

Every book that God gives me represents a grace act, as well as a faith-building exercise. Thus, I am humbled and amazed at His revelation for each new project. I am "Exhibit A" of the notion that "we have this treasure in earthen vessels, so that the surpassing greatness of the power will be of God and not from ourselves" (2 Corinthians 4:7). So, God should receive all glory for this venture.

Equally true, I proudly proclaim my absolute allegiance and full loyalty to my Savior and Lord. In Christ, I am cleansed, complete, calm, and collected. Daily, I find in Him renewal, refreshment, and rest for my soul. Every fiber of my being is connected and sensitive to His presence. Bless His holy name!

The revelation of truth regarding Christ emanates from the well-spring of God's Holy Spirit. The promised "Helper" teaches and brings to my remembrance salient insight from the Word of God, for the people of God, for the advance of the kingdom of God. What He speaks, I vow to write!

My faithful congregation—Pleasant Green Baptist Church, in Kansas City, Kansas—represents a rich laboratory for exploring, discovering, and sharpening Christ's mission of "making disciples." For more than fifteen years, we have enjoyed a spiritual love affair, with major kingdom impact as our objective. We aim for excellence (not perfection) through Jesus Christ. Many congregations may be bigger, but none is better!

My church staff (administrative and volunteer) are among the best anywhere. They help me pray, focus, dream, cover the saints, envision our future in Christ, pursue, soar, and achieve—for the glory of God. Thanks to all for helping to produce another high-quality book.

The Office of the Pastor invests intellect, expertise, emotion, vigor, wisdom, research, typing, marketing ideas, and more in these written pursuits. Bless you for another victory for God's kingdom enterprise!

The ever-fresh eyes of a prayerful, wise, caring, professional editor enrich a book project. Great gratitude to Sis. Helen Gray, for all she does in enhancing these works. We are on our way to the *New York Times* Best-seller List!

Countless treasured colleagues across America have, perhaps unwittingly, contributed to the success of this project. Many long conversations served as seeds of chapters, prompting me toward additional research, reflection, and revision. In the process, you helped me "get it right."

I also express deep appreciation to my publisher, Townsend Press. This spiritual family of Christian publishers is ably led by the Executive Director of the Sunday School Publishing Board, NBC, USA, Inc., Dr. Derrick Jackson. The entire team of publishing specialists, editors, graphic designers, layout people, and marketers has made this a much better work! Bless you, Rev. Debra Berry, for every call and text!

I celebrate an array of pastoral friends and trusted colleagues across America. Routinely, we share prayers, Scriptures, quotes, sermon thoughts, illustrations, burnishing our preaching/teaching/leadership. Many of their words, perspectives, and impressions fill these pages. To all, I am truly grateful.

In early 2015, just after this book was completed, but before it was published, within a span of one month, my sainted mother, Mrs. Ellen R. Jones, and my beloved stepfather, Rev. Luther Jones, were both called from earth to glory. I sincerely miss them, and must acknowledge their vital deposits into my life. May this book serve as a modest "return" on their investment in me!

Finally, I sincerely appreciate my family: wife, Jennifer; son, Jarvis II; and daughter, Jillian—for sharing me with the church, the nation, and the world. I trust that the completion of another book reminds you of all the sacrifices you make; and, I pray that you recognize my dedication to you, and to the Christian ministry.

INTRODUCTION

The contemporary Christian witness immeasurably suffers as too many godly, dedicated, distinguished, experienced, influential, wise, and substantive spiritual fathers are disconnected from younger Christian leaders. What could be a mutually beneficial, affirming, and reciprocal mentor-protégé relationship is too often squandered. I am saddened as critical insight and practical tools for navigating Christian ministry and the Christian life are available from these veritable founts of wisdom while younger clerics languish, parched of spiritual sustenance.

In too many cases, retired and active Christian "fathers" are disregarded as sources of biblical, theological, spiritual, moral, relational, personal, and practical counsel. Their advice is not pursued as many young, would-be theologians genuflect before the altar of modernity, as if there are no valuable lessons to be derived from decades of spiritual service to God and His kingdom cause.

When advice from spiritual fathers is not cherished or embraced, the results include horrific leadership debacles, imperiling the body of Christ and damaging God's kingdom cause through Christ. In light of ministerial collapse and leadership catastrophes and the collateral damage they bring to congregational life, thus stifling community engagement, someone will ask, "Why didn't he/she talk to his/her pastor before acting in that manner?" Much heartache and many headaches could be avoided if such a conversation were held.

In no uncertain terms, I am explicitly asserting the necessity of a paradigm shift where younger clergy intentionally seek out called, anointed, weathered, seasoned, and compassionate spiritual fathers. Let me state the matter early on: Every pastor (especially younger ones) needs a pastor! In some Christian circles, this father figure is often described as a "spiritual covering."

Amid shifting winds and howling adversity, with many leaders leaving the Christian ministry due to health failures, high stress, burnout, and frustration amid unrealized achievements, we need to enhance the bonds of mentor and protégé. These relationships, if successful, can be initiated by the younger, while being welcomed by the older. I envision the symbolism: sitting at the feet of a mentor as he pontificates the love, grace, and mercy of God shown in Christ Jesus. In the Word, the great apostle Paul had been "educated under Gamaliel" (Acts 22:3).

This pattern of learning while receiving divine impartation flows from the Scriptures, as they highlight mentor-protégé relationships: Abraham and Lot; Moses and Joshua; Eli and Samuel; Elijah and Elisha; Uzziah and Isaiah; Jesus and the Twelve; Peter and John Mark; Paul and Timothy; and Paul and Titus—among others.

My utmost concern in this book involves informing and raising lofty standards of Christian leadership, developing leaders who will be key influences in shaping the thrust of the body of Christ which, in turn, will strengthen God's kingdom imperative in Christ.

Moreover, we shall endeavor to cull gold nuggets of hardearned wisdom and precious gems of advice from spiritual fathers in hopes of shaping ministerial careers and pastoral legacies.

The research methodology undergirding this book entailed compiling a diverse list of spiritual fathers (men with at least fifty years in pastoral ministry, with the average age of seventy-five years, some with seminary training, while others learned through intense study, reading, and consecration before God), and then eliciting their responses to a questionnaire. That survey form included many topics of concern: current Christian worship, music, preaching emphases; ministry objectives; managing change; pastoral vision; personal morality/integrity; a reading list; personal mentors; lasting achievements; social/political/economic engagement; handling pastoral transition; and more.

Responses to survey questions and collected stories featuring these spiritual fathers will reveal encounters with God and His miracles, along with His sustaining grace. Others will reveal the keys to longevity in Christian ministry. Others will reference an eventful faith journey, including tough moments, tragedies, faultlines, and more. Still others will acknowledge missteps, flaws, and insecurities before recognizing God's internal evaluation of character and integrity.

The godly fathers chronicled in these pages evidence faith in God, spiritual depth, chronological maturity, fidelity to the divine call, and fervor for souls with a throbbing heart longing to advance the kingdom of God. Their dignity in Christ is measured in white hair, weathered faces, slightly stooped posture, slowed gait, rhythmic cadence, and a methodical manner.

Chapters will cover several critical concerns: praise for, principles from, paternity of, presence of, and protection by fathers along with models of ministry with a view to developing a healthy perspective of his significant role. Intermittently, I shall reference my own spiritual fathers as personifications of principles expressed.

Such men are endowed with the Caleb spirit (see Joshua 14), with an insatiable desire for taking another "mountain" for the glory of God. They possess an inexhaustible treasure trove of anecdotes, experiences, epiphanies, discoveries, and fond memories of the vagaries of the Christian life, as well as Christian ministry. In many cases, these fathers seem to have seen it all. Not much fazes them anymore. Now, they are secure in their self-identities. They are resolute in their approach.

As a seminary graduate, I have deep respect for professors, philosophies, and principles gleaned and gained from the academy. At the same time, many seminaries offer theoretical, esoteric, metaphysical truths divorced from congregational life, with lectures, books, themes, and discussions far removed from daily living by saints of God. Accordingly, I sense that we need today great theories, books, and concepts from acclaimed sources in the academy, along with finely honed wisdom of the fathers, to make Christianity in general and the Christian ministry in particular all it should be for the glory and honor of God.

With legacy evaluations by God soon to follow, they refuse to traffic in trivialities. Instead, they speak with heft, with profundity, with gravitas, giving heed only to matters with "eternal," "quality," "Christ," and "kingdom" stamped on them.

If much of current Christianity bows to trends, following the culture rather than shaping it, spiritual fathers stand as the corrective and the cure for all that ails the Christian witness. These fathers, when and where necessary, are quick to repudiate fun, fanciful, foolish, and frivolous fixations rampant in Christian circles. Today, when I am tempted to embrace some popular though specious idea, I can hear a father figure ask, "What is the meaning of this; and, if you do it, will it increase faith and dedication to God?" If I cannot answer that the notion will further the cause of the Christian Gospel, I immediately abandon the objective.

Conversely, when the situation calls for compassionate understanding, spiritual fathers illustrate another side: affirmation of God's restorative grace. From life experience, they know that God takes shards from painful episodes, assembling them into a tapestry of His mercy, giving life significance and substance. These figures epitomize the Galatians 6:1 ideal.

If in some small measure I can persuade younger clergy to "yoke up" with a spiritual father for the glorification of God, evangelization of the unsaved, edification of saints, elevation of society, and advancement of God's kingdom, I will have discharged my assignment from the Lord. This mentor-protégé connection, in my view, offers an untapped opportunity for optimized ministerial effectiveness in the twenty-first century.

This book, finally, will detail scriptural principles underpinning fathers' theories, while adding practical context for the challenges of contemporary witness for Christ.

1

The Provenance of a Spiritual Father

In developing any concept, it is crucial that we start at its beginning. The word *provenance* fits into that framework, as it means "the place of origin; how it all began; the initiation." For example, if museum curators want to authenticate a painting, they examine its provenance: Is this really a true painting by Picasso, Degas, Cezanne, Matisse, or Van Gogh? In a world dominated by beautiful counterfeits, it is imperative to discern the real. So we explore the identity, style, influences, and origins of a piece's creator. In like manner, we need to apply the same principle as we explore the "spiritual fathers" in early Christianity

The world in the immediate aftermath of the New Testament, first century AD, swirled with drama, speculation, rumor, and intrigue. Relative to the central figure in human history, from my perspective—our Savior, Jesus Christ—many were wondering as to the future of the movement connected with Him. His twelve disciples each carried an agenda (personal, political, and otherwise) without giving evidence of stepping to the fore for Christianity's perpetuation.

Of course, from the record in the the book of Acts, some scholars argue that the apostle Peter or the apostle Paul became the chief instrument for the transmission of the truth of God's gracious intervention in human affairs, offering reconciliation to humanity through repentance, faith, and embracing of the risen Savior, Jesus Christ. Peter, then, spread the Christian message through preaching and teaching in varied cities of the region, fulfilling Christ's Acts 1:8 admonitions.

In the book of Acts, chapters 1–12, Peter was prominently featured as the major catalyst for geographic expansion of the Christian movement. From Acts 13 through its conclusion, Paul took the larger role through missionary journeys and collateral writings to far-flung church communities.

Expanding the breadth and spirit of Christianity, literally and figuratively, Paul utilized a variety of means: travelling, preaching, and establishing churches across the then-known world—while placing leaders, to whom he would send important writings (epistles), for the church body's spiritual growth in Christ. In so many ways, therefore, the scope of "the Word made flesh" radiated throughout the world.

During the late first century to the middle of the second century AD, prominent voices arose, such as those of Justin Martyr, Ireaneus, Clement of Alexandria, Polycrates of Ephesus, Tertullian, and others. The "Patristic Period" took its name from the Latin word *pater*, meaning "father." Indeed, these were the original spiritual fathers, or the initial Church Fathers. Let us, then, examine their role in shaping early Christianity. (Clearly, my effort will serve as a brief, broad overview of these leaders. Whole books have been and will be written, examining their role in shaping Christianity while being crucial human instruments in its perpetuation. I refer readers to those resources, indicated in the bibliography.)

The following are some ways that the early Church Fathers were instrumental in building on the foundation of Christ for the church and the advancement of the kingdom of God through God's Son.

ESTABLISHING THE BIBLICAL CANON

Christianity, at the close of the New Testament toward the end of the first century AD, was at a crossroads. After Peter and the other apostles died, eyewitnesses to the Master's life and work became nonexistent. Lacking those who actually walked with Him, many controversies developed. Then Paul also made his transition to glory, with legend holding that Paul was killed at the behest of the Roman emperor Nero. It was, then, a period of intense doctrinal controversy, with many ideas, ideals, and institutions in flux. The period was dominated by emerging voices (theologians, writers, and teachers) grappling with properly interpreting all events associated with the unique Galilean, Jesus Christ.

As various manuscripts floated in the post-Resurrection era purporting to tell the story of Christ's purpose, life, teachings, miracles, and death and its circumstances, there was a need to separate the authentic from the specious. So God used these Church Fathers through writing, judgments, and advocacy to assist the fledgling Christian movement in sorting through the multiple claims. The theological concept supporting this drive sought to validate ancient orthodox Christian doctrine. In effect, these Church Fathers were the original "apologists," taking on early threats like Gnosticism (claims repudiating Christ's coming in the flesh).

This work of the early Church Fathers, in defeating incipient forms of heresy, was crucial to Christianity. Human relationships with the heavenly Father made possible by the resurrected Christ place Christianity outside mere religion. The fact of the eternal relationship with God meant that He reached down to humanity, rather than human religion reaching up to Him.

Through multiple means we will never fully understand, the providence of God working through the Church Fathers established the biblical canon of the twenty-seven books of the New Testament (from the gospel of Matthew through the book of Revelation).

UNANIMITY IN RECOGNIZING REVELATION FROM GOD

Moreover, the Church Fathers came together in various ecclesiological councils to pray, listen, read, weigh, thoroughly evaluate, and ultimately determine which of the collected writings should be included for the New Testament, which scholars refer to as the *canon*. This word means "rule, measuring rod, or rule of life." These spiritual fathers, leaders of varied bodies of saints, met in councils and were quite instrumental in reaching unanimity on what writings passed the test of authenticity.

The first test for a book's inclusion in the canon centered on its author's connection to an apostle of the Lord Jesus and proximity to the events described. So, naturally, the gospels of Matthew and John were recognized without much debate. The gospel of Mark had merit because Peter, for instance, was its source. The gospel of Luke claimed authority primarily because Luke utilized interviews with eyewitnesses.

As the Church Fathers evaluated the validity of writings, they were keenly aware of content, substance, inspiration, inerrancy, infallibility, and authority of its message. Did it present Jesus Christ as the Son of God, recognizing His deity, life, mission, miracles, teachings, sacrifice, resurrection, and advent, looking toward His promised return? If so, that proposed book led to surprising unanimity from the Church Fathers.

SOLIDARITY IN AFFIRMING CHRIST AS SON OF GOD, LORD OF THE CHURCH

At this crucial juncture of world history during the first century AD in the environs of Jerusalem, it was necessary that true Church Fathers affirm with certainty the Savior's identity. Without their confidence, clarity, and certainty, the Christ message of spiritual and personal salvation—believing that Christ died for our sins and was raised on the third day—would remain imperiled. So as men of dignity and devotion to God, this was not a time for indecision.

In the plan of God, we can see the pivotal role of the early Church Fathers as they helped the fledgling Christian witness understand its place in the world order. Indeed, the Christ message had always been for humanity all over the then-known world, rather than as a splinter sect of Judaism. Early Church Fathers, then, had to walk in solidarity in sharing the importance of Jesus Christ as God's Son and, potentially, Savior for all who would "call on the name of the LORD" (Romans 10:13).

The early Church Fathers were persuasive spiritual leaders serving as holders of a crucial baton, passing on what they received from those who walked with Christ in the flesh. Now, the succeeding generation of Church Fathers saw their responsibility as one of passing on a legacy of trust in Christ. Nothing noble or transcendent, such as Christianity, could be perpetuated if its initial adherents were confused as to the means of salvation. Their expectation was simple: provide new believers with a continuity of beliefs in the deity of Christ so as to assure others of the viability of faith in Him, resulting in dynamic life then, as well as eternal life (later).

The work of the early Church Fathers, to be sure, was predicated on the notion of solidarity in presenting Christ as Savior of the world and Lord of Christianity.

RECOGNITION OF SALVATION BY CHRIST ALONE

Within the cacophony of voices clamoring for recognition as authentic proponents of Christianity, there was the need for definitive sources as to the means of reaching the invisible, transcendent God. The early Church Fathers, therefore, articulated the firm, fundamental, foundational reality of Christianity: it was built on the vicarious death and bodily resurrection of the Son of God, in whom belief leads to atonement and justification before the almighty God. Since Christianity is predicated on Christ, the surest way to defeat its spread would be a frontal assault on the Son of God. These early Church Fathers set themselves to "contend earnestly for the faith which was once for all handed down to the saints" (Jude 3).

Thus, it was necessary that the early Church Fathers repudiate, eviscerate, and eliminate specious writings and incipient doctrines before they gained widespread traction in the world of ideas associated with normative Christian expression. Like those seeking to contrast the authentic from the counterfeit, their work entailed extolling the crucial truths affirming the identity, purpose, and ecclesiastical as well as cosmological significance of the Son of God. In classic fashion, these men served as the original Christian apologists, defending the Christian faith from myriad political, cultural, and religious attacks. If left unanswered, these attacks would dilute persuasive Christian truth, while inhibiting personal, institutional, and geographic expansion of the kingdom of God—with Christ at its center.

By every measure, then, the early Christian Fathers were a fundamental asset to the Christian cause at a crucial time in its germination, gestation, infiltration, and formation as a dominant expression of the means of human reconciliation before the grace of God.

From review of the writings of the early Church Fathers, we come away with a deeper appreciation for their insistence upon the centrality of Christ as the sole route to "peace with God." With considerable insight from God's Holy Spirit, the early Church Fathers knew that the stakes of worldwide evangelism (spreading the Christ message to all humanity) were too high to trifle with substitutes for the substantive message of Christ's triumph of death, hell, and the grave, all in pursuit of reconciliation before the heavenly Father.

REFUTATION OF SKEPTICS, CRITICS, AND DENIERS OF THE SUPERNATURAL IN CHRIST

With scriptural metaphors referring to the military aspect of Christianity ("stand," "fight," "weapons of warfare," "whole armor of God," and more), the early Church Fathers saw themselves as ordained generals. Under God, they were tasked with leading Christian armies under their command in a protracted battle against the adversary as he used unrepentant infidels, false teachers, well-meaning skeptics, virulent critics, charlatans, and varied enemies of Christ.

During a time of attack by critics and anxiety for followers of Christ, these fathers understood the importance of maintaining respect for the supernatural element of the life and ministry of Christ. If they allowed Christ to be viewed merely as moral teacher, ethical paragon, miracle worker, or world idealist without His supernatural core, He would have been regarded, at best, as a religious romantic, offering a utopian dream devoid of pragmatic engagement with an ugly, dysfunctional, perverted, warped world system.

The foregoing are just a few ways that the early Church Fathers established a firm foundation for Christianity. They planted "seeds" in rich, fertile soil, resulting in refutation of early Gnostic heresy, continuing through various church councils aiming to ratify Christian orthodoxy, culminating with codifying Scripture. Indeed, when properly analyzed, their work had a profound impact, one stretching through the Middle Ages into the rise of world powers with geographic expansion, coming into the Industrial Revolution, reaching the great World Wars of the twentieth century, and beyond. (Obviously, whole books have been written on individual early Church Fathers as determiners of the identity, shape, and contours of Christianity. My brief attempt has been to illustrate their value early in the Christian narrative, while positing that, more than tangential, spiritual fathers are fundamental to the advancement of the kingdom of God.)

2

THE PRAISE OF A SPIRITUAL FATHER

Among many spiritual traits, a father in the Lord must exemplify godliness, faith, good character, Spirit-led anointing, prayerfulness, discipline, wisdom, dignity, kindness, compassion, and engagement among those considered his beloved children. In 1 Corinthians 4, the apostle Paul wrote from the perspective of such a father to the saints of Corinth. This aspect of fatherhood means that, despite fleshly, partisan, selfish bickering, indicating spiritual immaturity, God demonstrates concern for the growth and maturity of saints in Christ. As maturity deepens, it enhances Christian behavior before the world. Indeed, Paul fully loved the saints of Corinth, despite their glaring inadequacies. Emerging from a gross pagan culture, these new converts to Christ brought strange ideas, mysterious ideologies, and damnable behavioral patterns.

Paul's love for the Corinthian saints moved him to chastise them when necessary, with strong admonitions to correct beliefs and behaviors antithetical to Christian principles. So throughout this book, Paul met their questions with biblical principles.

Interestingly, many first-century concerns—divisiveness, misinterpretation of Christ, spiritual growth dynamics, believers'

THE PRAISE OF A SPIRITUAL FATHER

rewards, moral decline, litigation before heathen courts, marriage/divorce/remarriage, foods consecrated to pagan gods, pastoral support, self-indulgence, Lord's Supper practices, spiritual gifts, love and order in worship, the essential Gospel message, financial stewardship, and more—are still of great interest in the twenty-first century. While sin changes its name, it remains a snare to God's people as they seek to advance the kingdom of God in human hearts.

Today, true spiritual fathers follow Paul's pattern of exhortation, with an extra degree of love, tact, and sensitivity. Specific to the myriad challenges clergy face in an increasingly complex world, they need someone who truly cares for their success in ministry. Without that someone (compassionate spiritual mentor) stepping forward, untold catastrophe may ensue in the calling to serve humanity in the name of Christ.

Indeed, if a contemporary young clergyperson wishes to benefit from the wisdom of a father in the faith, that person must deeply respect and acknowledge the elder's experience, exposure, and expertise in Christianity. In the same way that good biological fathers demonstrate love and compassion to progeny through dedication, presence, protection, provision, promotion, principle, and perspective, spiritual fathers offer the same.

The presence of a spiritual father was illustrated in Paul's frequent allusions to the pain of distance, which separated him from those he had led and nurtured in Christ. Reading his epistles, we note the pathos of a spiritual father. These heartfelt epistles to "sons" (Timothy and Titus) and far-flung congregations (Corinth, Galatia, Ephesus, Philippi, Colossae) represent valiant attempts to substitute for physical absence. Clearly, Paul joyfully accepted apostolic responsibility as a present parent, used of God in edifying the faithful in Christ:

I do not write these things to shame you, but to admonish you as my beloved children. For if you were to have countless tutors in Christ, yet you would not have many fathers, for in Christ Jesus I became your father through the gospel. Therefore I exhort you, be imitators of me. For this reason I have sent to you Timothy, . . . and he will remind you of my ways which are in Christ, just as I teach everywhere in every church. (1 Corinthians 4:14-17)

Am I not an apostle? Have I not seen Jesus our Lord? Are you not my work in the Lord? If to others I am not an apostle, at least I am to you; for you are the seal of my apostleship in the Lord. (1 Corinthians 9:1-2)

Thus, the entire range of Paul's epistles, then, involved buttressing the faith of those growing in Christ. He worked to assist them as they understood, appreciated, and implemented core biblical principles. His anticipated result involved lives of yielded obedience and willing compliance with God's directives. Then these embedded principles would lead to lives of significance and purpose, honoring and glorifying God.

At the same time, such biblical and theological principles would protect them (and us today) against the subtlety, wiles, and crafted wickedness of the enemy of our souls. In the overall plan, these critical values will extend the kingdom of God through the production of fearless Christian disciples.

Later, Paul crystallized the best traits of spiritual fatherhood: presence, protection, provision, principle, and perspective. In a long passage worthy of examination, he defined that caring spiritual father:

Are they servants of Christ?—I speak as if insane—I more so; in far more labors, in far more imprisonments, beaten times without number, often in danger of death. . . . I have been on frequent journeys, in dangers from rivers, dangers from robbers, dangers from my countrymen, dangers from the Gentiles, dangers in the city, dangers in the wilderness, dangers on the sea, dangers among false brethren; . . . Apart from such external things, there is the daily pressure on me of concern for all the churches. Who is weak without my being weak? Who is led into sin without my intense concern? (2 Corinthians 11:23, 26, 28-29)

Because biblical principles are best demonstrated through living persons' applying them, let me capture and celebrate the concept of spiritual fathers with a current-day application. I came to my present pastorate in Kansas City in 2000, moving from my native home of Los Angeles. Suddenly, I was physically disconnected from two spiritual mentors who lived and ministered in California. (Yes, phone, Internet, and social media were available; yet, face-to-face encounters give me and many others optimal benefit.)

Therefore, I sought out a new father in the faith, a new pastor. God led me to another father figure, Dr. Wallace S. Hartsfield Sr. He was (and is still) a well-known, well-regarded Christian leader in Kansas City. His background includes leading a great church fellowship for more than forty years with integrity, influence, and distinction. As a Christian pastor, leader, and community activist, he served on just about every city and state commission imaginable. Most weeks, he was quoted in the local newspaper as a keen observer, shaper of thought, and trusted voice.

Upon meeting Dr. Hartsfield for the first time, I introduced myself. He acknowledged me as a new pastor in the Kansas City metro area. I asked him to serve as my new spiritual father, my "covering" in Christ. He agreed, and there began another thrilling chapter in my spiritual journey of faith. I thank God that he opened his heart and life to me, serving as my "godfather" in the city. He introduced me to many persons, affording me many privileges as a new son in the faith.

Inasmuch as I value the Christian minister as the spiritual catalyst in fostering social and political engagement in a community with a social-justice agenda, Dr. Hartsfield was the ideal candidate as a father in the Lord for me. In consideration of all he was still doing, and because he showed every indication of continuing such a wide-ranging ministry, I wanted to serve in a similar "anointing" of community leadership.

Early on, I was tremendously blessed to receive an invitation to serve as guest speaker for the annual Kansas City Martin Luther King Jr. Birthday Observance Mass Meeting. This event usually brought together at least a thousand people, including political, economic, religious, and social luminaries. When I looked out over that august audience, I was immeasurably blessed to see my new pastor, Dr. Hartsfield, among it. I acknowledged him as a positive presence in my life. Whatever anxiety I possessed that night as a speaker in a new town was quickly dispelled by his warm embrace.

At fifteen years running, we have maintained a warm Christian fellowship. He has been guest speaker at our church for many occasions. For years, I was guest speaker for his congregation. He has shown himself to be a wise, steady, consistent influence in my life. Often, whenever he wants to share a vision with younger pastors, Doc, as I refer to him, has included me. I recall his idea for a group of interdenominational black congregations and pastors who would pool financial resources to invest in socially responsible stocks and mutual funds. This fund, placed in a black-owned bank, would serve as a means of fostering African-American economic development. He called the concept "Exodus Group," with the objective of increasing the influence of these congregations in American capitalism. Ultimately, we generated approximately $50,000 for such purposes.

Such progressive thought and spiritual teamwork, along with other works, have encouraged me in Christian ministry. Afterward, I told him, "Doc, I am proud to call you my pastor, because you are a leader among men; this kind of community leadership and activism stirs my heart."

A few years later, another pastoral experience we shared was quite challenging: I encountered a church-related matter that necessitated wisdom, insight, tact, and sensitivity. I called Doc for confidential advice because he knew a great deal regarding this matter and the parties involved. We held a private meeting. I explained what I felt God had led me to propose, which would bring the matter to a successful resolution. We thoroughly discussed the matter, with his praying for me and the congregation. He added his wisdom and experienced pastoral perspective.

Afterward, I asked him to attend the meeting as my guest and as my pastor. He was concerned that some might misinterpret his presence, as Baptists hold to the "autonomy of the local church." I assured him that, nevertheless, he was welcomed, and his perspective would aid the overall issue/discussion. It was one of the best moves I could ever have made. We resolved everything, defusing a volatile situation, with God gaining the victory!

In hindsight, I was glad to benefit from his vast knowledge, perspective, leadership, and experience. Had I been arrogant, foolish, and rash, relying solely on reason, wit, charisma, and theological training, I could have seriously compromised my long-term leadership, prudence, and effectiveness. Also, without this father's steady hand and good judgment, it could have undermined our ministry as a Christian fellowship.

Throughout the last thirty years of Christian ministry, in my view, many clergy have fallen prey to unchecked hubris to their detriment.

My own challenge reminds me of the necessity of younger Christian leaders' calling on the blessings of fathers in the faith. Paul's narratives of the books of 1 and 2 Timothy and Titus represent inspired writings to his spiritual progeny. Indeed, it is a case of a Christian luminary conveying deep truths to leaders in their own right. Yet, within these epistles there is a poignant connection between mentor and protégé: "Paul, an apostle of Christ Jesus . . . To Timothy, my true child in the faith" (1 Timothy 1:1a, 2a).

Or note another sense of the relationship: "Paul, a bond-servant of God and an apostle of Jesus Christ, . . . To Titus, my true child in a common faith" (Titus 1:1a, 4a). The "true child" designation confirms a symbiotic, spiritual, sustained relationship. Let us meet these young biblical leaders.

Timothy hailed from Lystra (see Acts 16:1-3), with a Greek father and a believing, devout mother and grandmother. He had been led to faith in Christ by Paul and then became his loyal disciple, friend, and co-laborer. Although Timothy was chronologically young, he exhibited godliness, integrity, faith, and dedication to God and to his father in the faith. In many New Testament references, he ministered with Paul in several important venues: Berea, Athens, Corinth, and Jerusalem. The measure of their work together and Paul's confidence can be ascertained through the frequent allusions to Timothy in Paul's writings.

In the Pastoral Epistles addressed to him, Timothy served the church at Ephesus. Clearly, this young clergyman was able to handle sensitive, significant assignments with character, dedication, and excellence.

In that Ephesus venue, Paul admonished Timothy, a neophyte in Christian leadership: "Let no one look down on your youthfulness, but rather in speech, conduct, love, faith and purity, show yourself an example of those who believe" (1 Timothy 4:12). In a Greek culture which placed great value on age and experience, Timothy, a mere lad possibly in his thirties, would earn parishioners' respect as an exemplary disciple of Christ. Because of his long association with Paul, Timothy may be viewed by saints as wise beyond his years. I personally identify with Timothy as a Christian leader, as I served my first pastorate beginning at the age of twenty-two.

In the crucible of tough, stressful ministerial leadership, Paul offered an additional word from God: "But flee from these things, you man of God, and pursue righteousness, godliness, faith, love, perseverance and gentleness. Fight the good fight of faith; take hold of the eternal life to which you were called, and you made the good confession in the presence of many witnesses" (1 Timothy 6:11-12). While false teachers gravitate toward material obsession and loving money, Paul exhorted Timothy to live by a higher moral, spiritual, and intellectual standard. Because Christian ministry reaches beyond mental capabilities, confronting the timid, Timothy must "fight the good fight of faith," agonizing with the demands of Christ.

In a Christian "fight," a struggle for righteousness, one needs to integrate concentration, discipline, and extreme effort if one hopes to prevail. Further, the "good fight of faith" means sustained spiritual conflict against Satan and his kingdom of darkness. Empowered as a "man of God," Timothy (and other anointed clergy) had the internal resources to succeed.

Likewise, we discover Titus ministering for a period with Paul on the island of Crete; later, he was left behind there to continue and strengthen the work, providing spiritual care for the saints. Also, Titus proved central to the missionary work in Corinth, with mention of his name and the value he brought to the Christian expansion there at least nine times in the book of 2 Corinthians. This young elder demonstrated familiarity with false teachings that threatened the Christian movement. On Titus's résumé, he had earlier accompanied Paul and Barnabas to the Council of Jerusalem (Acts 15) to counter such heresy.

Thus, having proven his capabilities in spiritual service, Paul offered him all the necessary resources for effectiveness as a dedicated, Christian pastor: "For this reason I left you in Crete, that you would set in order what remains and appoint elders in every city as I directed you, . . . But as for you, speak the things that are fitting for sound doctrine" (Titus 1:5; 2:1).

Although the epistle is a brief one, it epitomized Paul at his best, writing to a young protégé/pastor. The apostle reasoned that if he could give personal encouragement and counsel to an inexperienced though well-trained and faithful leader, it would resonate within that fellowship, while radiating beyond it to other leaders. Then Titus would evaluate and appoint the next generation of leaders. In the glorious process, God would bless thousands of saints.

Thus, today, Paul's wisdom conveyed to both Timothy and Titus should be regularly taught, memorized, and rehearsed before a new generation of younger clergy.

Leaders of the contemporary Christian church especially need such reminders as uncertainty engulfs wide swaths of the body of Christ, irrespective of denominational ties. New ministerial assignments are commonplace. Yet, those fresh from the academy, full of optimistic—though yet unproven—theories should, at least, consult with some well-respected, noted father figures in their local communities.

For many reasons, I aspire to serve God and His church in the manner of Timothy, Titus, and others. Similarly, I aspire to engage with a latter-day Paul, a godly father of the first magnitude.

Joyfully, then, I add Dr. Wallace Hartsfield Sr. to a small group of fathers who cover me in spiritual grace, patience, love, and nurture. With a healthy sense of my own uniqueness I have, at the same time, drawn infinite lessons, both in life and leadership, from my personal mentors. I assert that God makes each of us as originals, yet we are all influenced by those we admire.

So I encourage all younger clergy to function as the best leaders they can be, fully appreciating those who have shaped their mental and moral development.

Unwittingly, early in Christian ministry many will mimic the words, mannerisms, walk, and analysis of a godly mentor. This should be expected. In time, however, it should lessen as the minister becomes comfortable in his own skin. Like David's being unable to function in Saul's armor, so the young cleric will be unable to use all that rightfully belong to the life of a mentor.

Facing internal uncertainty, Paul had an additional insight for Timothy: "Guard, through the Holy Spirit who dwells in us, the treasure which has been entrusted to you" (2 Timothy 1:14). The treasure, the Gospel message of Christ, proves too precious to neglect, existing in "earthen vessels" (2 Corinthians 4:7).

What Paul shared is precisely the benefit accruing from a father in the Gospel. After years of dialogue, training, and tutelage, Timothy knew by experience that he could always depend on Paul to proffer both a timely and timeless word of hope, guidance, and exhortation.

In my case, I did not receive a written epistle from my spiritual fathers (the late Dr. E. V. Hill, the late Dr. A. H. Newman, the late Dr. Jessie Dawson, or Dr. Wallace Hartsfield Sr.); yet, I did hear similar admonitions to faith, faithfulness, and fidelity to the Lord.

In every case, I highly value all they conveyed to me concerning living for and serving God and His saints. Salient truths they deposited in my spirit have become real as I internalized what I was taught. Embedded revelation from God became a lodestar for my life. In turn, in a thirty-six-year (and counting) Christian ministry, I have shared thoughts of insights with others.

When intelligent, gifted, anointed, caring younger Christian leaders celebrate these fathers, they provide invaluable benefit to themselves and the people God calls them to serve. Indeed, it should be quite simple: younger clergy should take great examples from fathers, honed in yesteryear, while adapting the jargon of today against current challenges, all the while grounding actions in the Word, centering in Christ, relying on the Spirit of God—all for the extension of His kingdom cause.

To be sure, some are dissuaded from seeking or using godly advice from fathers because many contemporary clergy are convinced that their challenges are novel and unique. From my perspective, I would counter that too often the nomenclature of vexation changes while the underlying malady—estrangement from God due to sin—remains constant throughout all time.

Further, many young ministers fail to celebrate godly wisdom similar to those advising young King Rehoboam (see 1 Kings 12). In that painful episode, the king sought advice from both elders and from his peers. Unfortunately, the king repudiated wise counsel from the elders, instead following unproven, unsound, unscriptural, questionable counsel: "But he forsook the counsel of the elders which they had given him, and consulted with the young men who grew up with him and served him" (1 Kings 12:8). In the aftermath, the chronicler repeated the terrible truth: "The king answered the people harshly, for he forsook the advice of the elders which they had given him, and he spoke to them according to the advice of the young men" (1 Kings 12:13-14a). Incredibly, this lesson in unbridled hubris leads to the dissolution of a strong, united, productive kingdom. The takeaway from this ignominious episode should warn any would-be leader!

In light of the warm relationship between godly, biblical teams of mentors and protégés, the King Rehoboam debacle, and failures in Christian ministry today, it behooves younger clergy to rush to the warm embrace of spiritual elders in Christianity.

Beyond debate, I am firmly in the ranks of those appreciative to and blessed by spiritual fathers. Indeed, I cannot fathom my life, worship, witness, and ministry for Christ without such stalwart, steadfast, sterling characters as they marvelously modeled service to God before my eyes.

3

THE PURSUIT OF A SPIRITUAL FATHER

A friend once expressed frustration with the lack of wisdom by so-called leaders in the land. In the U.S. Congress, with 535 representatives of the people, we noted a yearning for competent adults in the room. While corporate America enjoys the exotic, promoting thirty-year-old CEOs amid youthful mania, we shared concerns for prudence and judgment. My friend further rued the fact that even in Christian circles, inanity and silliness were presented, celebrated, and commended, while national institutions are being undermined by the paucity of wisdom.

We agreed that while the general situation was deeply regretful, the greatest area for alarm was in the spiritual realm marked by the absence of wisdom, prudence, and competent influence. In a word, the Christian church today sorely suffers from the absence of sober judgment from spiritual fathers. These fathers should be vigorously pursued by younger clergy.

As the church of the Lord Jesus Christ increasingly suffers from a lack of wisdom among its leaders (the ability to hear from God, stand on His Word, synthesize timeless principles, and present profound guidance), it imperils all committed to God and His kingdom paradigm.

Particularly troubling today in the body of Christ is the growing proclivity among immature saints to mistake renown, verbal skills, creativity, and charisma for wisdom. To override these considerations, we must hitch our emotional, intellectual, and spiritual wagon to the Scriptures. There, we learn the singular importance of wisdom: "Acquire wisdom! Acquire understanding!" (Proverbs 4:5a); or, "But if any of you lacks wisdom, let him ask of God, who gives to all men generously and without reproach, and it will be given to him" (James 1:5).

To transmit a body of spiritual wisdom from God centering in His Son, Jesus Christ, so as to foster an eternal relationship with humanity, we sorely need seasoned proclamation of life-altering truth. In the main, spiritual fathers are charged with this critical task. Enduring wisdom from God passes to a spiritual father down to the next generation of spiritual leadership. It contrasts with political correctness, repudiating conventional wisdom and surveys of popular notions at any given moment in time.

Wise Christian leaders must never test their beliefs on the basis of who agrees with them. Wide acceptance of spurious ideologies may indicate shallow, insidious, amoral positions. God's called, anointed, effective leaders are not moved by opinion polls.

My late pastor, Dr. Edward V. Hill, renowned Christian leader, spiritual father, man of wisdom, and icon of the faith, always warned against embracing as fact assertions or notions made by someone—anyone—without analyzing them against the standard of the Word of God. Wisely, he urged me to seek to discover the perspective of Jesus Christ and God's kingdom in every matter.

Influential people (in varied fields) as such must not be affirmed as arbiters of right thinking. Rather, the moral, just, and honorable perspective alone comes from God, as He dictates irrefutable truth.

Indeed, the prophetic tradition in the Word of God warns against presenting a pleasing message: "'Do not be afraid of them, For I am with you to deliver you,' declares the LORD. . . . 'I am watching over My word to perform it.' . . . 'I have made you today as a fortified city and as a pillar of iron and as walls of bronze against the whole land'" (Jeremiah 1:8, 12b, 18a). The young prophet Jeremiah needed God's assurance of the validity of his calling despite age, inexperience, and personal frailty. Likewise, clergy today need divine enablement to achieve kingdom expansion. Most often, that enablement is channeled through fatherly wisdom.

Moreover, beloved Christian fathers are known for Holy Spirit anointing, integrity, credibility, character, commitment, professionalism, wisdom, keen insight, ability to carefully weigh ideas, and discerning long-term implications beforehand. Beyond dispute, godly fathers should not simply be affirmed on the basis of age, white hair, or years accrued in ministry. Instead, deference to a sainted father in Christ must be earned continually because of exposure, experience, excellence, intellect, dignity, spiritual analysis, trustworthiness, and profundity.

Like Enoch, such a spiritual father must walk with God (see Genesis 5:25). Pointedly, he must always exhibit conspicuous love for God, love for people, and concern for expanding God's kingdom through Jesus Christ. Character, integrity, devotion, and resolve will serve as remarkable hallmarks of his life and leadership paradigm.

Astute younger clergy, in my judgment, gain immeasurably from proximity to, and learning from, the kinds of spiritual fathers I feature throughout this book.

Let me offer another brief synopsis of one who greatly influenced me and the Christian ministry that God has been shaping in me since the beginning of my ministry. Over time, permit me to mention some mentors I pursued.

While serving as a young pastor in Los Angeles in the early 1980s, I sought out one of the most influential voices of that city—renowned AME preacher, Dr. T. Larry Kirkland. An outstanding preacher, visionary, builder, and spiritual leader, Dr. Kirkland was beloved as "the down-home preacher with the up-town message."

He hailed from Birmingham, Alabama, but fit perfectly in the mysterious mosaic of metropolitan Los Angeles. In the main, his nickname endeared him to thousands of parishioners and radio listeners.

Over his twenty years at Brookins AME Church in Los Angeles, God used his Spirit-filled, thoughtful, dynamic, warm, engaging messages to build a congregation of more than eight thousand congregants. When he sang "I Got a Feeling Everything's Gonna Be Alright," God caused troubles and crises to melt away! Christians across the city were blessed by his ministry.

Equally impressive, while giving priority to the spiritual, Dr. Kirkland envisioned, organized, and guided a tremendous outreach effort: providing food, clothing, counsel, housing referrals, job information, and free income-tax preparation assistance to disadvantaged L.A. residents. He was recognized by the political leaders there for his tangible, continual impact. In my view, Dr. Kirkland wonderfully wed the dual foci of Christian ministry—in the cathedral and in the community.

Once in the midst of what to me was an existential challenge threatening my future effectiveness as a minister, I went to Bishop Kirkland's office. In the best sense of a spiritual father, he allowed me to pour out my heart. With tender kindness, he affirmed me as a young, questioning leader. His wise counsel has served me until this very day: "Keep praying, keep preaching, keep pressing—God will bring you through." I am very proud to call him one of my gospel heroes. On countless occasions, we have shared the joy of a Paul-Timothy spiritual fellowship as mentor and protégé.

Affirming the hand of God upon his life, the African Methodist Episcopal Church elected Dr. Kirkland as its 114th Bishop, in its quadrennial session in Louisville, Kentucky, July 1996. I was privileged to share in that session.

While I have never lost track of Bishop Kirkland as a spiritual father, a major mentor in my life, acknowledging his godly influence, treating him with the utmost respect, I remind him that I, even though a Baptist, helped elect him: I gave his campaign the grand sum of $100 (smile); and persuaded hidden Baptists to support his cause!

Too many times to mention, I have observed Bishop Kirkland exhibit faith in God (deep) and love for people (matchless), share personal resources (unusual), and offer kind words (unsolicited), all the while assisting others to become what God ordained for them.

What continues to amaze me is that once such men reach lofty heights of Christian ministry, they often become aloof from those who are not their peers. Instead, Bishop Kirkland and others of his ilk are emotionally secure. Accolades and applause do not define them. They know that fame is fleeting, while seeing people transformed by Christ is eternal. They have reached the point of working for the advancement of God's kingdom cause with all else paling in comparison, falling into insignificance.

After God relocated me to serve my current congregation in Kansas City, one of my special invited speakers was Bishop Kirkland. His message was timely and well-received by our church family. It was a singular joy of mine to royally host him in the manner that he had embodied for me. On every occasion of conversing or seeing one another at a conference, I am tremendously blessed by his wisdom, insight, vision, resolve, and influence for the kingdom of God. The Christian witness would be greatly enhanced in every way if more spiritual fathers fulfilled their calling, as does Bishop T. Larry Kirkland.

At the same time, I have been immeasurably blessed by an ecumenical spirit. Thus, another font of wisdom over the years has been Bishop Charles E. Blake, pastor of West Angeles Church of God in Christ in Los Angeles, and presiding bishop of the international COGIC family.

While a young pastor in Los Angeles, I attended one of Bishop Blake's early worships (he led four!) on countless occasions before heading to my own. His godliness, wisdom, preaching, administrative gifts, and love for humanity always served as the best example. I was struck by the scholarship, anointing, charisma, depth, and spiritual character reflected in every message he delivered.

On multiple occasions, he invited me to his office, at which time we would discuss ministry concepts. That he would take an interest in me (at the time serving a small congregation) made a major impact, by which I am still overwhelmed. Sensing some favor from God, with grand dreams I invited Bishop Blake to speak for our $100 per plate fund-raising dinner. And, guess what? He accepted! (For any doubters, I have the picture of us from the event in my present office.)

The West Angeles Church led by Bishop Blake optimized ministry in Christ through a wide variety of community engagements: private school, bookstore, performing arts theater, senior housing facility, counseling center, Bible college, and more than two hundred other ministries. Most impressive, even as brick and mortar do not reveal the full mystery of God, thousands celebrate a modern-day Christian mecca in West Angeles Cathedral, a five-thousand-seat, multilevel oasis of divine grace, a splendid worship setting, sacred space for the glory of God as He intervenes in human life through His Son, Jesus Christ.

In truth, more than once I have been intimidated by one who leads a congregation of some 25,000; yet, he always made time for an eager, questioning, yearning young clergyman such as myself.

Equally true, God wonderfully used Bishop Blake to build both a dynamic congregation and a national presence. He is a Gospel giant in terms of twenty-first-century Christian engagement—from city hall to the state capitol, all the way to the White House. With a ministry outreach in Africa, he also has achieved global distinction.

While I am sure he has been flustered at points, Bishop Blake consistently epitomizes a man of spiritual composure. Watching him closely over more than thirty years, he exudes equilibrium of focus before God: never too low, but always operating in excellence. One who searches the dictionary for a man of faith, a unique man of God, need not be surprised to find Bishop Blake's picture there as an example of the concept.

Most astonishing, from my perspective at least, Bishop Blake stood before a major COGIC gathering in Kansas City and referenced me as "My friend, Jarvis Collier." My colleagues present were overwhelmed. (After the buttons on my shirt came off, I returned to my ministerial composure.) The takeaway from every encounter with Bishop Blake has been simple and profound: maintain the centrality of Christ in your calling to serve humanity.

As the leader of an international Christian fellowship, Bishop Blake has a tremendous responsibility to serve as spiritual father to millions the world over. He provides love, grace, insight, and vision for thousands of missionaries, musicians, ministers, pastors, elders, superintendents, and bishops. Some 50,000 regularly attend the COGIC Holy Convocation each year in St. Louis, Missouri. "Official Day" climaxes that session, with the message brought by Bishop Blake.

In 2014, when I preached the Word at his church, he honored me (after a long day of leading saints in worship) by personally coming to the evening worship. At seventy-four years of age, all would have forgiven him for skipping that one night. Yet, he led us all in praise dancing before the Lord! I reminded the fellowship that, as far as national ministerial exposure went, I was ready for the Rapture at that moment!

A third major "father" voice I embraced and enjoyed in Los Angeles was Bishop Benjamin Reid of First Church of God. This mountain of a man preached with erudition, anointing, and clarity. Indeed, in the preaching moment he was drenched on his first point!

The congregation he led, First Church of God, was a mammoth one, with several thousand congregants who met in multiple Sunday morning worships. Those times were punctuated by vibrant, rollicking, dynamic, Christ-centered, anointed, prayerful worship.

As a visitor, I found them to be particularly empowering, as they highlighted praise singing, with the Word of God delivered by a powerful servant of God. In the best tradition of a dedicated pastor, Bishop Reid was successful in blending biblical scholarship with practical application, giving worshippers something tangible to which to aspire.

Equally true, Bishop Reid was a spiritual visionary, a leader far ahead of his time. Bishop Reid's vision, moreover, involved meeting actual needs of those beyond sanctuary walls.

Accordingly, First Church of God, through off-site properties, served as a site for a private, first-class, amenity-filled elementary/middle school (rigorous curriculum, technology, uniforms, and high expectations), highly acclaimed Bible college/seminary for graduate students, Christian bookstore, and prayer center, amid a variety of ministries.

Indeed, it was a tough time for many of us when God called home Bishop Reid in the late 1990s. I recall attending his Celebration of Life. It was a God-centered, Christ-exalting, worshipful occasion, with several of his spiritual progeny seeking to approximate Bishop Reid's scholarship and verve. In the aftermath of his life, we cherish his family and those continuing his legacy of ministry and engagement.

A fourth source of spiritual inspiration was the late Dr. Thomas Kilgore of Second Baptist Church of Los Angeles. He shared many of the same traits of those featured previously: scholarship, dignity, and ministry sensitivity, all within the kingdom motif centering in Jesus Christ.

Second Baptist Church, under Dr. Kilgore's stewardship, offered high church worship and social-justice emphases within an historical and relevant context. At almost any worship or conference, premiere African-American leaders might address the congregation.

Spiritual wisdom from father figures like Bishops Kirkland, Blake, and Reid; Dr. Kilgore; and my own pastors Dr. E. V. Hill and Dr. A. H. Newman, must now be transmitted to younger, eager, questioning protégés. Picking the brains of spiritual elders in the faith represents an exercise in sincerity. The information should be received, processed, and implemented at the first opportunity for successful results. In these moments, God provides spiritual epiphanies.

In the feedback loop, as younger clergy express gratitude for pearls of wisdom, it prompts fathers in the Lord to plumb the depths of their life experiences with God for additional insights to share; and the process continues.

Though I was then—and still am—a Baptist, Bishops Kirkland, Blake, and Reid became sources of great counsel to me. Unwittingly, they taught me the grandeur of God: He is Sovereign— bigger than Baptists alone. Indeed, all who call upon Him in the name of His Son, Jesus Christ, are welcome to grace, mercy, and love!

This spiritual relationship of fathers and sons in the Christian faith should resemble a flowing fountain and a thirsty imbiber.

From the father wisdom pours forth; and for the son, questions are answered. The younger now armed with acquired wisdom has doubts cancelled, anxieties abated, plans made, and leadership established. Indeed, a large part of who we are has to do with the people (mentors) who have influenced us. If fathers fail to unlock the doors to truth, they forfeit the opportunity to radically change others' lives.

The need for wisdom in the Christian witness has never been as great as at the present moment. Established congregations are repudiating long-held Christian principles, sacrificing them on the altar of expediency. Christian leaders are running frantically toward the newest trend, following the latest fad, embracing the current "hot" idea. Regrettably, many do not find contentment in standing on the Bible as the inspired, inerrant, infallible, unassailable repository of God's revelation.

We need some settled spiritual fathers who will remind younger Christian clergy of our legacy in Christ. Biblical concepts such as humanity's lost condition, grace, mercy, faith, salvation by the blood of Jesus, sanctification, sovereignty, justification, imputed righteousness, heaven, hell, and eternal judgment must serve as sufficient scaffolding for a life of dynamism in Christ.

When tempted to proclaim a "fluff" message in the interest of acclaim, spiritual fathers serve to remind younger clergy of our holy calling from God. Indeed, we have been entrusted with undeniable truth grounded in Jesus Christ. In any analysis, it represents a profound message. That message must be preserved and perpetuated for future generations.

Serving as someone's spiritual father by divine assignment involves a weighty proposition and godly responsibility. The seminal text in this regard reminds us of this: "For if you were to have countless tutors in Christ, yet you would not have many fathers" (1 Corinthians 4:15a). Paul, then, made a critical distinction between *tutors* and *fathers*.

A tutor in New Testament times was an attendant or custodian, usually a slave whose job was to assure safe passage for a child of privilege to school, relieving the family of anxiety or concern. This tutor/slave was important, though not vital, to the life of the child.

Fathers, in an infinitely greater way, were related to the child, exercising primary responsibility for his/her safety, provision, education, and ultimate destiny.

How is the power of a spiritual father felt?

1. **INTENTIONALLY CONNECT WITH SPIRITUAL PROGENY**

Specifically, then, spiritual fathers' responsibilities are quite vast. Fulfillment of these tasks require countless hours of prayer, Bible study, counseling, answering questions, dispensing advice, correcting error, and providing for (and in general being a faithful presence in) the life of an impressionable child in the faith. At its best, this unique relationship may sprawl across years, or even decades. Like any organism, it matures over time. It will be fed by love in Christ, intentional nurture, patience, forbearance, and constant reciprocity, in the process becoming mutually beneficial. Sons (and daughters) in the Lord keep spiritual fathers fresh, keenly aware of the challenges of Christianity in an ever-changing, twenty-first-century culture.

As I have stated before, and will emphasize throughout, the mentor-protégé relationship must be initiated by the protégé who seeks information and inspiration. Emotional, psychological, and volitional wisdom will only be dispensed to the degree that a protégé seeks it from a caring mentor. In the process, the mentor determines the sincerity of the protégé by the latter's willingness to listen, learn, laugh, and live within all that has been given to him or her.

2. HELP A PROTÉGÉ DISCERN SPIRITUAL REALITY AMID INFORMATION OVERLOAD

The twenty-first-century world presents varied opportunities for accessing new sources of knowledge. This generation of preachers, for example, has every tool known to humankind for researching and grappling with Scripture en route to its proper interpretation. Everywhere there are assets for learning Hebrew (Old Testament concepts) and Greek (New Testament notions). Indeed, many sermonic presentations veer too much toward the head while others veer too much toward the heart. Instead, we need a balanced approach to biblical interpretation, one culminating in our Savior, Jesus Christ.

Wise fathers, spiritual mentors in the Christian faith, meanwhile, help younger clergy members distinguish between technical knowledge and practical knowledge. Christian seminaries do well in conveying technical knowledge: worship principles (honor), biblical languages/history (heritage), principles for interpretation of Scripture (hermeneutics), and sermon preparation (homiletics).

At the same time, wise, older craftsmen transmit practical knowledge: serving God, loving parishioners, cultivating core values, and living by steady habits. By example, they teach the importance of focus, developing patterns of personal and professional discipline, morality, integrity, patience, and the significance of experience. "Been-there, done-that" beats lofty dreams every day.

3. TALK TO THOSE WHO WILL LISTEN; THEN LEARN THE WAY OF RIGHTEOUSNESS

As I reflect on a riveting Christian ministerial journey covering nearly forty years, I recall the joy of sharing in denominational gatherings. There, a beloved father in the faith might "hold court," surrounded by young clerics. Every word he uttered was received as if it were the voice of God. Once he pronounced a concept, all would later affirm it as definitive. This was a favored venue for encountering national legends of the Christian faith.

Other opportunities for dissemination of wisdom within the African-American preaching tradition were granted during the former Bishop College (Dallas) Ministers Institute and the Hampton University (Virginia) Ministers Conference. The spiritual fathers we encountered there were, in my view, refined raconteurs.

As esteemed craftsmen of the pulpit, even in small settings, they could regale listeners with quips, witticisms, stories, and experiences. Insightful books, sermon seedlings, preaching topics, ministry ideas, philosophies of pastoral success, and encouragement emerged from those moments in the presence of giants of the Christian Gospel. (As I have remarked in several chapters of this book, I was tremendously blessed to meet some of the African-American luminaries of the Christian pulpit during the last half of the twentieth century and the early twenty-first.)

In the biblical tradition of "Iron sharpens iron, So one man sharpens another" (Proverbs 27:17), we find consolation. This generation of clergy, in my judgment, needs to take advantage of the sharp edge of ministerial fathers in Christian ministry. Forged on the anvil of a loving mentor, many protégés will reach their full potential.

4. THE VALUE OF LONG-TERM PASTORATES

An invaluable lesson from a senior statesman in the faith (spiritual father) might well be the critical key to a long pastorate within the same congregation. In other words, pastoral influence, sway, and ability to direct the thrust of a Christian fellowship increases with the advancement of years served there. Not surprisingly, leaders who have served a congregation for, say, thirty years have far greater clout than those in their first five years of a tenure.

Getting to really know parishioners (their struggles, stresses, and situations), pastors are enabled to better minister to them with compassion, patience, and grace. Long pastoral tenures in the same place make it easier for a leader to "sit where they sat," knowing their hurts, sufferings, trials, and misfortunes. So esteemed, well-established fathers bring unique perspective to the task of leading a congregation.

A pragmatic way to achieve a long pastorate, indeed, involves avoidance of scandal, conflict, and controversy. Find a comfortable niche, a particular specialty (evangelism, visiting the sick, Bible studies, prayer focus, kindness to children, spiritual counseling, social-justice advocacy, theological reflection, and so forth), and flourish there. During times of adversity, those in a congregation who have experienced pastoral expertise in a particular arena will tend to laud a pastor for steadiness and continuity in that aspect of ministry.

Indeed, within several Christian traditions and denominations, some pastors are very weak in preaching while compensating for that preaching deficiency in, say, soul winning, prayer, building a grand edifice, or enlarging the membership rolls. Conversely, some Christian leaders have weathered church storms by the grace of God, congregational love, and their unparalleled preaching gifts.

One wit I know, with fifty years' pastoral experience, always counsels wise choices before church conflict develops, rather than effective strategies once such occurs. Of course, even the best leader will face challenges simply because the Adversary initiates it to thwart God's kingdom progress. (I remind myself often that our Savior faced extreme censure from the religious leaders of His day.)

5. TEACH LASTING SPIRITUAL, BIBLICAL, DOCTRINAL PRINCIPLES

Meanwhile, wise fathers must tether younger clergy to the essentials of the faith, maintaining priority in what honors God, celebrates Christ, seeks the Holy Spirit, and resonates in God's Word while edifying saints for the enlargement of the kingdom. Of necessity, these lessons ensure biblical accuracy and theological orthodoxy. At their best, spiritual fathers work to frustrate the all-too-common tendency of the enemy to divert younger clergy away from central truths, moving them to marginal, though interesting, concerns. Yet, as many traffic in the trite, trivial, and tangential, the essential, enduring, and eternal are lost.

Today when I hear simplistic, pragmatic preaching and teaching in the vein of motivational or inspirational speaking, I wonder, "Where are the men and women of spiritual wisdom?" Surely, when spiritual fathers are present, alert, and concerned for the Master's kingdom enterprise, they will be alarmed by the diminution of the Christian message. Trivial preaching, inevitably, will produce trivial saints of God. And the result will be further erosion of the Christian faith as a spur for redemptive transformation in the world. Within this matrix, many will miss the monumental mission of the Master: advancing the kingdom of God through Christ in human hearts.

6.   CHANCE ANGERING AND FRUSTRATING A PROTÉGÉ

The dissemination of wisdom from spiritual father to younger clergy may take an unusual route: *provocation* to *frustration* to *germination* to *inspiration*. Each leg of that journey exposes younger clergy to questions, followed by more questions. This "interrogative" method, often instigated by a caring, dedicated father, will culminate in grand discoveries. (While the method is played out, young clerics deign to say, "Enough already with the questions; please, just give me the answer!")

In time, however, as one trusts God, ideas form, ideologies congeal, identities develop, and insights emerge. In the dynamic of thrust and response, many find their originality in Christ, rather than becoming a bad copy of another. The best Christian fathers, then, seek sons (and daughters) to surpass them.

The godly mentor, of course, is not overly concerned with the perfection of the product as much as with the purity of the process.

Sadly, protégés who are only fixated on product lose sight of their progress along the process. Athletic coaches, seasoned by years and experiences, know that the process is well worth the struggles involved, especially as those committed to it will, inevitably, reach a place of maturity and lasting achievement. Therefore, coaches (mentors) preach the value of good habits ("Just get better."). Similarly, in the ways of God's kingdom, spiritual fathers must refocus clergy on "getting better" in all aspects: worship, prayer, Bible study, reading, reflection, discipline, integrity, dedication, vision, striving, commitment to excellence in Christ, and heightened expectations.

7. RECOGNIZE THE SIGNAL HONOR OF IMPARTING TRUTH TO ANOTHER LEADER

The calling from God upon a spiritual father represents an invaluable honor. I note spiritual transference in Paul's writing: "The things which you have heard from me in the presence of many witnesses, entrust these to faithful men who will be able to teach others also" (2 Timothy 2:2). In these sweeping words, God's Holy Spirit anointed Paul to reference four Christian generations: Paul; Timothy; Timothy's protégés; and their protégés. Now as the teaching extends the results are astounding, blessing thousands of saints in the process, all for the glory of God through Christ.

8. GRACIOUSLY AND GRATEFULLY RECEIVE HONOR FROM A PROTÉGÉ

When protégés recognize the value of mentors, often the former will bestow public commendation on the father in the faith. Such honor might be conveyed through some small act: a timely letter, a warm phone call, a purchased suit, a necktie, cufflinks, cologne, a pen/pencil set, a financial gift, paying for a nice dinner, or a range of other grateful acts. The specific act is not as important as this acknowledgment to a spiritual father: without you, my ministry in Christ would not have its heft, width, depth, longevity, trajectory, or meaning.

When I assess my Christian leadership, I sincerely regret that I did not have sufficient time to "load" my spiritual fathers with material benefits. (Each died too soon, in my judgment.) Instead, I vow to pass along the spiritual nuggets they bequeathed to me (this book represents my gift to their memory).

9. PROPERLY EVALUATE A GODLY MENTOR

It should be clear, then, that an avuncular, experienced, perhaps curmudgeon figure represents my ideal of a spiritual father, dispensing wisdom directly from the throne room of the heavenly Father. This father in the faith patiently passes the torch of responsibility for spreading the Word of God, with its apex in the Lord Jesus Christ, to those following afterward.

Unashamedly, I celebrate godly fathers toughened by decades spent in obedience to God, fulfilling their calling, still seeking to embed a spiritual legacy in a generation of Christian clergy too often enamored by overnight success, on a precarious trek to instant acclaim.

Instead, I contend, long-time Christian ministers need a godly champion—a caring, ardent advocate. Successful godly leaders embrace spiritual fathers, well-meaning pastors who pass down well-honed wisdom.

In a world of near-obsession with youthfulness, that goes to extreme lengths to exhibit vitality and perkiness with the sense that anyone over fifty must be on the descent of functionality, we immeasurably benefit from wise persons, especially father figures. We need these fathers to counter prevailing Christian opinion, which holds that the message is best delivered by a contemporary leader honed by events of this decade. Regrettably, such notions leave little space for those with spiritual, biblical, and life perspective spanning back to antediluvian days, like the twentieth century!

10. A COMMENDATION OF SPIRITUAL "SENIOR STATESMEN"

As a closing reference to fatherly wisdom in matters of God's kingdom, I recently noticed a riveting picture in our local black weekly newspaper. It captured images of three "senior statesmen" of the Christian pulpit, standing together at a community event. I marveled at the combined years of Christian leadership, preaching, and teaching they embodied. Collectively, they probably represented more than 150 years in service to God. It is doubtless that over those decades they had faithfully led congregations, proclaimed the Word, prayed for countless parishioners, stood with the weak, counseled the troubled, given hope to the despairing, and, in general, represented the name of the Lord, Jesus Christ.

During their ministries, these fathers had witnessed tremendous change in the community, nation, and world, impacting the Christian witness. Indices of progress had mixed with reasons for sadness. Through it all, their godly wisdom had given congregants and the community at-large a basis for faith, courage, and determination. As champions of biblical, spiritual, moral, and ethical transformation, they placed humanity on a heightened trajectory.

Over the years, we believed for better days because God used these men to buoy our hopes. When dreams were shattered, wise fathers encouraged us to keep the faith. When tempted to curse our circumstances, wise fathers counseled a different course. Thank God for their wise application of biblical principle, along with pragmatic and strategic insight.

Moreover, their godly wisdom has immeasurably blessed thousands of saints, to the glory of God. With meager resources, they built lasting community institutions for the benefit of parishioners and those outside the spiritual fold. As I evaluate Christian fathers' legacies, in the vernacular of the urban core I utter, "We owe you, big time!"

4

THE PATERNITY OF A SPIRITUAL FATHER

The notion of paternity references the central role a father plays in bringing life to another through the fertilization of a woman's egg—a biological fact. In the natural realm, it represents a signal honor to serve as a father. Of course, biology does not reveal the entire story, for true fatherhood encompasses the Word, psychology, sociology, and theology.

Often in clearly dysfunctional settings, there is controversy as to who is actually a child's biological father. Television talk shows trivialize what should be a very personal, moral, ethical, and serious matter as the couple and the studio audience await paternity test results.

Right-thinking, value-laden men, by and large, are quite proud of their children as they emerge from a committed, godly, harmonious relationship. Christians honor God by having children within the bounds of sacred marriage, as verified by Psalm 127:3-5. Indeed, there is infinite joy in one's progeny as the DNA from the father passes to his children, giving infinite possibilities.

At the age of thirty-two, with the birth of my son, I was tempted to pass around cigars in celebration of seeing my name continue into the next generation. It indicates lineage and legacy. On the other hand, as the father of a daughter, there is a singular delight in reading to and praying with a beautiful angel at bedtime!

Indeed, there must be more for a true father to achieve. Any man can sire a child, provided he is of normal health. Instead, a father raises his child or children to become mature adults. The process is painful, costly, time-consuming, exasperating, and life-draining, but when done well, it is a joy like none other!

For Christians, the best formulation comes from Scripture: "Behold, children are a gift of the LORD, The fruit of the womb is a reward. Like arrows in the hand of a warrior, So are the children of one's youth. How blessed is the man whose quiver is full of them; They will not be ashamed When they speak with their enemies in the gate" (Psalm 127:3-5). A godly father, then, represents several roles: provider, protector, promoter, priest, and powerful presence.

As I shift to the particular emphasis of this book—spiritual fathers—I pray that all will hear and sense my frustration with the endemic of "fatherless families" among the urban, gritty, low-income, African-American cohort. Increasingly, the church of the Lord Jesus Christ, with compassion and yet moral outrage, must address this ongoing problem with biblical, spiritual, moral, and pragmatic solutions.

For our purposes, God has placed spiritual fathers in the body of Christ with the serious responsibility of serving as spiritual coverings for younger clergy as they embark on an eventful journey of self-discovery, maturing to serve individuals, congregations, and institutions within God's kingdom.

Many seminary professors, theorists, and role models will impact young, impressionable clergy, as well as others within the wider culture. Greater exposure to these sources can have positive and negative effects. Yet, the anointing of the spiritual father remains a unique one. Our Savior, Jesus Christ, the supreme example of

Christian ministry, did not execute a single ministry act except as a Son in reliance upon His heavenly Father.

So in the supernatural realm, God superintends the entire process whereby a spiritual father receives sons (and daughters) in the Christian faith. Often, younger clergy commence their ministries for Christ under a particular man's leadership, care, and long-term influence. The mentor-protégé phenomenon must never be viewed as happenstance, accidental, or haphazard.

Rather, God brings the two together, infinitely developing the younger. In a special way, God aligns passion, purpose, potential, temperament, ideals, vision, and kingdom focus. As these reciprocal relationships grow, the father recognizes loyalty to God, dedication to Christ, integrity, demonstrated respect, curiosity, desire for spiritual depth, and other intangibles. A godly father celebrates good traits while patiently and lovingly correcting bad ones.

On the other hand, the son yearns for a father's spiritual covering, indicative of caring, compassion, experience in Christian ministry, prayerfulness, adherence to Scripture, and substance, all for the glory of God.

In biblical revelation, God makes Himself known to Abraham (see Genesis 12), marking the man as patriarch, father to many succeeding generations. Interestingly, in the divine plan, God's promise to Abraham came when he was childless. Indeed, the ways of God defy human logic and rationality. Later, covenantal blessings to and upon the people of God would flow through the channel started with the patriarchs Abraham, Isaac, and Jacob, affirming a line of spiritual fathers. So, spiritual fathers matter!

In the New Testament, esteemed rabbis (revered and respected for their extensive knowledge of Judaism's laws, rituals, customs, rules, mores, traditions, feast days, and more) were often called "father." Note the halting respect in the voice of Nicodemus (see John 3:1-4), as he approached Jesus Christ. Though ignorant of the chasm between religion (staid Judaism) and relationship with God (dynamic Christianity in Christ), Nicodemus would soon learn the meaning of being born again through the love of a new father, Jesus Christ.

Over the two millennia since the time of Christ's earthly ministry, the Christian movement has been augmented by ecclesiological leadership, from the Roman Catholic Church (for example). Those leaders, referred to as popes, cardinals, monsignors, bishops, archbishops, and priests (called "father"), all serve to bless the Christian family. Within other Christian denominations, similar titles hold for servant-leaders. In Christianity, however, titles do not guarantee that the holder meets his qualifications; instead, service to God, His kingdom, and reaching lost humanity characterize true spiritual leaders, both official and unofficial.

Spiritual fathers, in the main, seek to pour themselves (hopes, dreams, experiences, failures, lessons) into progeny—examining motives and aspirations, deceits and self-deceits, pride, shame, and unexpected nobility. Throughout the process, godly fathers grade these "exams" so as to gauge clergy potential. When and where they discover such potential, mentors cultivate it. At its best, Christian ministry, then, approximates an apprentice, with younger clergy learning while working under and alongside a more insightful, seasoned, and weathered practitioner of the ministerial craft.

In so many ways, trusted, venerated, and experienced spiritual fathers will leave an indelible mark on their progeny. Both in time and in eternity to come, these fathers will be recalled as seminal figures whose imprimatur was well-established in discernible worship, prayer, study, comportment, dedication, and vision for advancing the kingdom of God through Christ. Truly, spiritual fathers are granted favor from God to serve in such an influential capacity.

Within the revealed biblical tradition in the Old Testament, we note a distinctly beneficial arrangement: Israel's liberator, Moses, modeled godly, faithful, trusting, obedient commitment to God. Moses' protégé, Joshua, mimicked these attitudes, while aligning his own life toward the Creator. In other cases in Scripture (as with Elijah and Elisha, for example), significant transfers of wisdom flowed from the father in the faith to the spiritual son.

Equally true in the New Testament, our Savior mentored twelve inquisitive, faltering, doubting, yearning, contentious disciples. Even with daily miracles and manifestations of divine power, the Master often raised a pointed inquiry: "Where is your faith?" Or He would chide them: "O, you of little faith." These questions remind us that a father's faith should surpass that of those younger in the ways of Christ. Christian discipleship is best conveyed to others when fathers display trust in God despite tough times, taxing circumstances, loss, pain, and suffering. Such brokenness affirms God as the ultimate healer.

Part of my thesis, therefore, involves the unseen potential in sharing the grace of God with all humanity. And when a young man or woman expresses a sense of the divine call to Christian service, it should be viewed as a monumental undertaking. Such a spiritual father will never know the future plans of God for that son or daughter in ministry. Thus, all clergy are precious in the sight of God and should be nurtured with fatherly love, care, and affection.

An older colleague, Apostle Aaron Royster of Chicago, and I discussed this spiritual mentoring concept. He emphasized that, in truth, this special bond between mentor and protégé should represent a supernatural, mystical, God-ordained one. He referenced the apostle Paul's exhortation to the believers in Corinth: "For if you were to have countless tutors in Christ, yet you would not have many fathers, for in Christ Jesus I became your father through the gospel. Therefore I exhort you, be imitators of me" (1 Corinthians 4:15-16).

Indeed, though, while many may apply for the role of tutor in Christ, younger clergy can have only one spiritual father. The present generation of Christian leaders celebrate a number of teachers (who sponsor conferences, preach nationally, and write books), but not many true fathers (those able to usher sons and daughters into their full potential in Christ).

Every young Christian leader should avoid fastening his/her life to just any spiritual father, and vice versa. The relationship must be sanctioned by God, taking into account personality, background, temperament, sensibilities, intellect, character, integrity, and life vision. When all those qualities converge, it signals the beginnings of a successful relationship in Christ. In this regard, Bishop T. D. Jakes said, "It is a tragedy for sons to misalign themselves to someone who cannot speak to their destiny."

God's revelation of spiritual paternity must have relevance for the entire body of Christ, encouraging the kingdom enterprise through Christ. Paternity must also resonate specifically in the hearts of Christian leaders, whether they lead under the label of Anglican, Catholic, Assemblies of God, Baptist (all varieties), Lutheran, Methodist, Presbyterian, Church of Christ, Church of God, Church of God in Christ, Church of the Nazarene, AME, AME Zion, Pentecostal, Apostolic, Word of Faith, Primitive, Independent, Fundamental, or non-denominational.

These denominational labels may stymie some, but in the main, they reflect the rich diversity of God's people; saints of God are not monolithic in worship styles, sanctuary sites, preaching modality, vestments, congregational size, race, ethnicity, language, culture, budget, locale, or any other man-made distinction. What unites us, however, as Christians involves affirmation of and affinity with the risen Savior, Jesus Christ.

In the foreknowledge of the Savior, He prays for the church, His body, "that they may all be one; even as You, Father, are in

Me and I in You, that [the world] may believe that You sent Me" (John 17:21). Indisputably, spiritual fathers hasten such functional (though not actual) unity, via favorable encounters with impressionable younger clergy.

More than anything, denominational labels should never distract the Christian family from its paramount kingdom-of-God mission: reaching the unsaved through redemptive relationships residing in Jesus Christ. Leaders and adherents of groups named may fixate on buildings/budgets, programs/personalities, meetings/mega-mania, form/functions, without addressing their responsibility to God as agents of mass spiritual and supernatural transformation.

Tragically, this world system interprets the multiplicity of labels as misplaced in-fighting among those who should unite as one in Christ (see John 17:21-23). Amid world challenges (terrorism, volcanoes, earthquakes, economic turmoil, personal anxiety, and moral laxity), many simply want real-world answers!

Full disclosure: I am indebted to Dr. Mark Hanby, a stellar spiritual father, for writing a great book: *You Have Not Many Fathers*. In it, he offers rich wisdom, insight, passion, and revelation from God. Rather than claim ownership or originality for what I have learned from his book, I will rather quote liberally from his thesis. I would highly recommend Dr. Hanby's book for all who seek even greater depth on this subject of spiritual fathers in the body of Christ.

In the seminal teaching on spiritual mentors (see 1 Corinthians 4:14-16, written above), this congregation would not be a model to emulate (rife with pettiness, partisanship, feuds, fornication, dysfunction, disorder, egotistic exhibitions of spiritual gifts, lack of love, and more). Yet, out of that mess, God gave them (and the body of Christ) a profound message.

What lessons on spiritual paternity might be derived for us today?

1. GODLY IDENTITY RESIDES IN CHRIST

Too great an emphasis on any leader aside from Christ inhibits advancement of the kingdom of God while negating the mission of reaching new souls. Famous preachers are, at best, yielded vessels for sharing saving truth in Christ. Greater, the message ("God was in Christ reconciling the world to Himself") from the vessels must be given the highest priority. So it devalued Christ for Corinthian congregants to claim, "'I am of Paul,' and 'I of Apollos,' and 'I of Cephas'" (1 Corinthians 1:12). Instead, all deference went to Christ, even as God chose to affirm Him through called, anointed, sent servants, mere instruments in God's hands.

2. IN GOD'S PLAN, LEADERS FOCUS ATTENTION ON CHRIST

Paul boldly admonished the unruly Corinthian saints precisely because of his paternity of them in Christ: "Therefore I exhort you (as your father), be imitators of me" (1 Corinthians 4:16). Black spiritual fathers understood this relationship, with the esteemed Dr. C. A. W. Clark of Dallas telling young preachers, "The Church belongs to Christ through headship, and to you through stewardship." Such wisdom means that Christian pastors/under-shepherds earn the right of leadership through continual service to God's people with loyalty and devotion in the name of Christ.

Within the pastoral role, Christian leaders are able to impart spiritual truth from the Word of God, with Christ as the apex of such divine revelation. Most successful leaders, then, received insight from a spiritual father. It is the order of God to pass such wisdom down from father to son. Note Paul's words in another place: "For this reason I remind you to kindle afresh the gift of God which is in you through the laying on of my hands" (2 Timothy 1:6). That verse usually references the Christian practice of ordination, where a council of ministers examines one's biblical knowledge, personal character, moral integrity, and scholastic preparation for full-time Christian ministry. If the council so judges one ready for the rigors ahead, the minister will be ordained, after they literally lay hands upon him or her. In a very real way, the laying on of hands references a symbolic transfer of divine grace from one called, anointed minister to another.

Generally, the length of a spiritual father's leadership model, ministry, experience, or pastorate coincides with his influence in that ministry or institution, and in guiding younger clergy. In spring 2015, Lyle Schaller, esteemed Christian writer, theologian, and church prognosticator, passed away after a lengthy global ministry, with many possessors of his books. (I own at least ten Schaller texts myself!)

3. FOCUSED IN CHRIST AND FOLLOWING LEADERSHIP, THE CHURCH HAS IDENTITY

Dr. Hanby teaches on this point:

Paul knew who he was and why he was given his place in God. It was the Corinthian church that was not receiving Paul's fatherhood and had no true father to follow. As long as a congregation or ministry stays out of God's order, the people will have disorder and lack identity. If we are without a (godly) father, then we have no name, no identity, no heritage, no inheritance, and no true brethren.

Later, Hanby reminds us, "The organizations of God's kingdom should be modeled after His Word, not the principles of this world. The church is more than a franchise on the street corner; it is more than a preacher's union. The church is to be the representative of kingdom truth in the earth."

I agree with his assessment, adding that the church distinctly represents an organism with the life of Christ coursing through us, intentionally bringing humanity to new life, hope, and behaviors.

Indeed, Hanby makes that point well: "The purpose of the church is to be an outpost for the kingdom, not a man-made, man-patterned, and institutional, bloodless machine that produces programs and numbers, but not sons and daughters."

In the 1 Corinthians 4 reference, Hanby reminds us,

Instead of having many fathers, they had ten thousand instructors. The word for "instructor" here in the Greek is *paidagogus*, which means "boy-leader." This term refers to a servant whose official position was to make sure the children were educated. Thus, fathers were substituted by hired servants unrelated to spiritual inheritance.

4. **SPIRITUAL FATHERS RESEMBLE NATURAL ONES, ONLY BETTER!**

In the natural realm, fathers are necessary for safety, solidarity, and stability for wives, children, and families. Accordingly, a family without a father suffers financially, socially, relationally, psychologically, and spiritually. Without their presence, provision, and protection, fatherless families fall under oppressive conditions. In the natural order, fathers' absence in families leads to poverty.

Conversely, in the spiritual realm, Hanby informs us, "Oppression occurs when immature rulers serve as babysitters over congregations, leading the people without any true vision. 'Where there is no vision, the people perish' (Proverbs 29:18a)." Also, he adds an important caveat: "We need so desperately to belong, to have boundaries, to know who we are in God. An orphan will seek for many years for any information he can find concerning his heritage, for without a family line he will never really know himself."

Presented with this biblical and practical foundation, we understand much better the vital role of establishing paternity from spiritual mentors in the body of Christ.

5. **SPIRITUAL FATHERS AND SONS ALIGN IN SPIRIT AND HEART**

Several years ago, God healed me of a benign brain tumor. After being released from the hospital, I felt God's strong impression on my life. He gave me a word, "father," and the compelling sense that I was incomplete unless I gave that covering of compassion to spiritual sons (and daughters) in Christ. Along with care, that covering would entail impartation, reorientation, gravitas, and ultimate priority to the kingdom of God.

I resolved then to offer everything I had to those sons and daughters who would understand my spirit and trust my heart as their spiritual father. Indeed, the revelation from God frightened me because it was for my sons, my church family, and for my city. The last aspect of it was particularly troubling because many Christian leaders in my city were (and are) considerably older than I am. Understandably they would, therefore, resent my trying to tell them anything about God! Nevertheless, I know what God placed in my spirit. So I am available to those who can accept my spiritual covering.

In the context of 2 Kings 2:1-14, we note this crucial connection through the prism of Elijah (father/mentor) and Elisha (son/protégé). Hear Hanby again: "There must be a sharing of a common vision, an endurance of relationship, and faithfulness to God and to each other in both father and son for inheritance to be transmitted. . . . With cascading mantles and cries of 'My father, my father,' the connection between spiritual generations is complete."

6. **SPIRITUAL PATERNITY IS AFFIRMED AS SONS RECOGNIZE THEIR FATHER'S "VOICE"**

Due to the nature of the relationship of spiritual fathers and sons, with God's kingdom advancement predicated on impartation in Christ, a son or daughter in ministry must place his/her life into the hands of a spiritual father. If, for example, Timothy was to reach his full potential in Christian ministry, it would ensue from his yielding his life to Paul. Respect, deference, and vulnerability toward a father in the faith exemplify openness to information, inspiration, and impartation. It represents a central quality of trust that a child has in his father. This close relationship fosters sharing of challenges, mistakes, and imperfections as well as hopes, dreams, and desires in an atmosphere of security.

When I reach glory, after worshipping God, if He so allows, I must thank my spiritual fathers for their voices of love and graciousness to me. Indeed, I heard that voice, and it blessed me. At so many intervals, they endured my immature questions, impulsive assessments, rash choices, and ongoing frustrations as God used them to mold me in the image of Christ for God's glory and advancement of His kingdom.

Not all Christian clergy will discern who should establish paternity over them. In other words, not all clergy recognize the voice of their spiritual father. Consider Hanby on this point:

> With misplaced zeal, some launch into a shopping spree for spiritual fathers, improperly pursuing headship. . . . Others pursue directions unauthorized by the Spirit, endeavoring to be joined to an organizational structure or denominational headquarters in lieu of a father's covering. Still others wander the aisles of the charismatic smorgasbord with empty carts and checkbook in hand, looking for brand names in colorful packaging. . . . The truth is that fathers are not chosen from directories or bought from catalogues.

Hanby continues with the following:

> A spiritual father is someone whose life and ministry raised you up from the mire of immaturity into proper growth and order. A spiritual father is the one whose words pierced beyond the veneer of a blessing into the very heart and

marrow of your existence, causing massive realignment to your spirit. He is the one who rescues you from the doorstep of your abandonment and receives you into his house, gives you a name, and makes you his son."

Relative to a certain "voice," our Savior began His ministry after a sublime word from heaven: "This is My beloved Son, in whom I am well-pleased" (Matthew 3:17). Similarly, Christian leaders today should not begin ministry with any expectation of success until the voice of a godly father is spoken in the earth.

Equally true, I have several colleagues who have done well in ministry but, I am afraid, they exist without paternity. They are gifted but act as orphans, moving from one influential figure to the next, depending on their whim. They lack security because they have not yielded to that unique voice of a spiritual father.

Finally, Christian leaders know their earthly paternity because they connect with Christ who, in turn, connects with the heavenly Father: "he goes ahead of them, and the sheep follow him because they know his voice. A stranger they simply will not follow, but will flee from him, because they do not know the voice of strangers" (John 10:4b-5).

5

The Presence of a Spiritual Father

What a privilege God affords to one made alive in Christ, called by God, anointed by God's Holy Spirit, assigned by divine providence, compassionate in nature, godly in character, devoted by desire, loving by design, and engaged by practice. I reference one unique man serving as a spiritual father to another, often in the context of serving a Christian congregation, seminary, denomination, or organization.

This spiritual mentor, as a spiritual father made wise by years, brings to the table his perspective of observations, research, achievements, and experiences, becoming a seminal presence in those God has spiritually birthed into Christian leadership. As with an obstetrician, he is deeply appreciated for bringing the baby to birth, clearing its breathing passages, wiping its after-birth, cutting its umbilical cord, and exposing the child to its full functionality and life potential.

Heightened, in the supernatural realm, God superintends the entire "birth" process, whereby a spiritual father receives sons (and daughters) in the Christian faith. Often, younger clergy commence their ministries for Christ under a particular man's leadership, care, and long-term influence. The mentor-protégé phenomena must never be viewed as happenstance, accidental, or haphazard. Rather, God brings the two together, infinitely developing the younger. In a special way, God aligns passion, temperament, ideals, vision, and kingdom focus. As these reciprocal relationships grow, the father recognizes loyalty to God, dedication to Christ, demonstrated respect, curiosity, desire for spiritual depth, and other intangibles.

On the other hand, the son (or daughter) yearns for a father's "spiritual covering," indicative of caring, compassion, experience in Christian ministry, prayerfulness, adherence to Scripture, and substance, all for the glory of God.

In biblical revelation, God made Himself known to Abraham (see Genesis 12), marking the man as "patriarch," father to many succeeding generations. Interestingly, in the divine plan, God's promise to Abraham came when he was childless. Indeed, the ways of God defy human logic and rationality.

Later, covenantal blessings to and upon the people of God would flow through a channel started with the patriarchs, "Abraham, Isaac, and Jacob," affirming a line of spiritual fathers. So, spiritual fathers matter!

Their presence in the lives of younger clergy serves to direct the latter in the mysterious ways of God. Most Christian leaders celebrate the one who led them to saving faith in Christ; encouraged their early ministry endeavors; honed them in faith principles; assisted them in difficult times; and more.

In the New Testament period, and shortly afterward, esteemed rabbis (religious authorities, seen as spiritual fathers) were well-known and respected for their command of the Jewish Torah (the first five books, primarily of the Old Testament). Because of their superior knowledge and leadership on matters pertaining to what was allowed versus disallowed in the Law, they were held in very high esteem by their students and followers, and the religious masses. Indeed, in various times in Jewish history, it was customary for persons to stand up in honor of an entering rabbi.

As Christianity spread into the Middle Ages, respect for spiritual leaders (males) was affirmed as an indisputable reality. While there was much to discover in the hierarchy of Christianity among its many branches, as more of the world was discovered, conquered, and settled, we know that spiritual fathers greatly influenced each succeeding generation of leaders. Indeed, the advancement of the kingdom of God as the name of Christ was more widely shared owes a debt to strong, courageous, insightful spiritual fathers.

In AD 1054, the Great Schism separated the Christian church into Western (Latin) and Eastern (Greek) branches, recognizing Western Catholicism and Eastern Orthodoxy. Even as doctrinal issues buttressed this division, the leadership of either branch was male, and the principle of spiritual fathers was further embedded into the Christian culture.

In Christianity, at the same time, titles should not represent the most important consideration; instead, service to God, His kingdom, and reaching lost humanity represent transcendent, paramount concerns. Note the admonition from Scripture: "It is a trustworthy statement: if any man aspires to the office of overseer, it is a fine work he desires to do" (1 Timothy 3:1).

The Protestant Reformation, though radically analyzing doctrines by repudiating lifeless tradition and hollow religious practices, did not diminish the importance of spiritual fathers in shaping the Christian trajectory. Reformers especially edified Christian clergy, challenging them to give ultimate priority to Scripture. Martin Luther, John Calvin, John Knox, and others used their influence as fathers in the faith through reliance on the Word of God to unusually shape the forward progression of Christendom.

At times, I have wondered, "Who was the person responsible for leading young boys like George Whitfield, Billy Graham, Billy Sunday, T. D. Jakes, or Joel Osteen to saving faith in Christ?" Obviously this anonymous individual—a mere human instrument through whom God worked—could not then know that the one he brought to salvation would one day himself lead millions more to that same Savior, Jesus Christ.

What does the presence of a spiritual father produce in progeny?

1. SECURITY

Christian leaders in a close, meaningful, healthy, affirming relationship with a spiritual father will undoubtedly find themselves secure in conversing with him because he has repeatedly demonstrated his concern, love, and compassion. When persons experience security, they are able to share successes and failures in an atmosphere free of judgment, censure, and shame. "I blew it there" represents a true reflection of one's state of mind when discussing an awful decision made in the past. The human tendency to avoid responsibility must also be taken into account when entrusting oneself to one whose love is unquestioned. Even if others turn away, a spiritual father lives in daily recognition of his paternal responsibilities. Living out this concept requires a personal touch.

As I have and will do throughout, I praise God for the presence of spiritual fathers in my life. In this context, I am extremely thankful for godly mentors. Let me reveal a few details of a painful divorce I went through years ago.

As I talked about it, two fathers stoically listened in love. As a young Christian minister, I was ready to resign from Christian leadership, feeling that I could not represent the heavenly Father in the name of Christ with such a serious blemish on my personal integrity. My marriage did not dissolve because of infidelity, or drugs, or abuse, or any external challenge; rather, we were simply unable to reconcile two distinct worldviews. Worship, prayer, biblical counseling, or larger family intervention could not heal the breach, I am saddened to add.

The men I most trusted advised me to stay in my ministerial calling, continuing to share the Word of God. For several months, through tears, I soldiered on. In the midst of that emotional brokenness, I found strength from God to continue onward. I also found that those who heard my testimony of God's restorative grace could identify with me, as God yet offers another chance. None should, however, take God's grace for granted; yet, God sent Christ to the world for sinners and, through His shed blood, we are all cleansed!

2. SELF-CONFIDENCE

The presence of a spiritual father, moreover, reminds his progeny of at least one critical, determined, engaged "partner" in the Christian calling who serves God and humanity in the name of Jesus Christ. Christian leaders who are self-confident achieve much more in life than those unsure of a spiritual support system. Some glide through life fully assured of the mentor who, in current vernacular, "has their back." That is, nothing detrimental will happen to one who maintains contact and conversation with a spiritual figure of renown. The individual rests in this knowledge, as does the wider world.

In the African-American Christian tradition, it is commonplace to hear a reference to one as the "boy" (no matter his age) of some prominent spiritual father. Rather than a put-down, this term serves to alert all that the ways and attitudes of the father are probably shared by the son in ministry. In other words, it represents an affirmation of a spiritual relationship equal to or greater than the natural one.

In the Old Testament narrative of 2 Kings 6, we discover the need for confidence in a young, untested, fearful servant to the mighty Elisha (who had been molded and mentored by Elijah).

Here, we recognize the transfer of spiritual wisdom: "So he answered, 'Do not fear, for those who are with us are more than those who are with them.' Then Elisha prayed and said, 'O LORD, I pray, open his eyes that he may see.' And the LORD opened the servant's eyes and he saw; and behold, the mountain was full of horses and chariots of fire all around Elisha" (2 Kings 6:16-17). Self-confidence arises from a trusting spiritual father's believing in another's inherent potential.

In the absence of a godly father, progeny may feel vulnerable to strong personalities in the church pews, other colleagues, or the world at-large. With due respect for the gifting of others, God's grace activated through spiritual mentors helps me feel good about my own place in the kingdom of God.

3. PERMISSION TO EXPLORE PARAMETERS OF CHRISTIAN MINISTRY

Because of the presence of spiritual fathers in my life, on more than one occasion I have been emboldened to try something that I discerned as the will of God for my life. Akin to the self-confidence matter above, I felt that with their emotional support, guidance, wisdom, and engagement, I could relocate to the Midwest to assume a pastorate, marry a beautiful, talented wife, have a child, write books, and lead a church in varied ministries. As I articulated my objectives, they never once applied brakes to my ambitions. Instead, as they heard my plans, they enthusiastically offered ways to make those plans come to fruition, adding ideas that I had not considered.

In our conversations, they ratcheted up the stakes of the undertaking. In a way, they invested in my dreams, taking co-ownership and responsibility for their outcomes. If I had failed in a venture, at the very least it would have been with the guidance of a supportive father figure.

Let us enlarge on this notion. Younger clergy should never be dissuaded from an undertaking by a spiritual mentor. When neophyte leaders entrust their lives, ministries, and futures to another, that spiritual father should encourage the protégé to dream big dreams! If the protégé dreams of moving beyond parochial, insular, shallow concepts, it will be fostered in large measure by a caring, godly mentor. Again, when someone we trust believes in us, we tend to believe in ourselves.

In the natural realm, one of the benefits of a biological father's presence, say, at a baseball or basketball game in which his child is a participant, is that it encourages that child's progress on the diamond, on the field, or in the arena. So the Christian witness today could immeasurably benefit from some fearless cheerleaders for the spiritual enhancement of younger clergy as they aspire to advance the kingdom of God through the Lord Jesus Christ.

4. COURAGE TO EVEN FAIL

Though not a godly, sensitive, holy man (as he ultimately trusted in self, rather than God), King Saul of Israel, a mighty warrior, in 1 Samuel 31:6, died with his sons: "Thus Saul died with his three sons, his armor bearer, and all his men on that day together." Saul's damnable epitaph reminds us of the fact that, in the natural sense, sons will remain with fathers of questionable judgment, simply because of biological ties. Among Saul's sons, Jonathan knew of God's displeasure with his father, nullifying Saul's leadership of Israel and giving it to Jonathan's friend David (see 1 Samuel 20:13ff). Though Jonathan's love for Saul persisted, his soul covenant with David was sacrificial, selfless, enduring, and deeply moving.

In Christian ministry, younger clergy must discern the optimal time for a move, often without clear and definitive information. In these times of uncertainty, it really helps to have a godly father present and accessible so as to give assurance in the venture. In short, success in life comes by way of having special people there for us, just in case we have some reservations regarding a new initiative. After talking with them, most of our fears are allayed and doubts settled as the way is made clear for us.

Often, monumental plans are shelved, imperiling the advance of the kingdom of God through Christ because many convince themselves of impending failure without exploring potential problem areas with a trusted, older, wiser, more experienced father figure.

5. BRANDING ONE'S PROGENY

A crucial role played by a prominent and present spiritual father involves his ability to influence one leader, or many following after him, in the way of branding his personality there. If one is a keen observer, it quickly becomes apparent when a Christian leader has been nurtured and developed under the shadow of a more dominant figure. In every way, this godly relationship should be celebrated for its lifetime benefit, especially from the perspective of the younger party.

In Acts 22, the apostle Paul reflected upon his life arc. He recalled the positive influence of the well-regarded, eminent rabbi Gamaliel. In this man's instruction, Paul found nuances of wisdom from the Old Testament Law. In fact, these lessons formed more than the basic foundation for Judaism, as practiced by strict adherents who constituted the Sanhedrin Council. These lessons proved preparatory, however, for the life-transforming revelation he received from his Damascus Road experience with Jesus Christ. What occurred there marked his life for time and for eternity.

The intricacies of the Law which Paul learned from Gamaliel served him after his conversion experience because, in the foreordained plan of God, Paul composed a great portion of the New Testament record. In that record of Christian expansion, we note Christian mission and engagement, fostering God's kingdom and engulfing new Christ followers in a dangerous, hostile, Christ-averse world. Indeed, Paul's analytical, argumentative (in a positive sense) reasoning, and intellectual capacities were honed by time under Gamaliel's tutelage.

Now, God would use those capacities in affirming the risen Christ as Savior of the world as Christ followers share redemptive truths. The presence of new converts across Asia Minor and the then-known world attested to the powerful presence of a godly mentor as he influenced Paul who, in turn, would influence Timothy, Titus, and others. This fact validates the maxim, "The fruit doesn't fall far from the tree."

6. THE INEXTRICABLE UNION OF PROVISION AND PRESENCE

It is nearly impossible in the natural realm for a biological father who is present in the home not to provide for his family. Indeed, when he eats he will automatically purchase food for all those under his care. Similarly, when he shops for clothing, he will ensure that all the family is well-stocked with necessities. The same holds true in providing some type of housing with utilities paid, furnishings, appliances, and more. Not surprisingly, he will insist that children attend school. Good natural fathers see, sense, and serve their family's needs. Often, he does this even before they express such needs.

With the men of our congregation, I champion fathers as ultimate providers, doing all within their power to ensure that their families' multiple needs are met. All of these ideas are normative for a present, provisional father.

Thus, I am advocating the same sensibilities for a spiritual father. Under the power of God, he should provide his progeny with all that is necessary for ensuring good spiritual habits (worship, prayer, Bible study, faith, devotion, discipline, and obedience), a safe environment, encouragement for intellectual development, and more. If necessary, he will discover ways to supplement financial costs for Bible college studies or theological matriculation fees for a young student under his care. By all means, let us repudiate the foolish notion of "Nobody helped me; he should go to school the best way he can."

When I speak of a godly father's provision, I am acutely aware of its importance. Let me cite two examples.

I went off to seminary with the explicit financial aid of my home congregation with the full encouragement of my pastor, the late Dr. Edward V. Hill of Los Angeles. He proclaimed and modeled his own credo: "The call to preach is also a call to preparation." He delighted in having more than a hundred sons in ministry. If they qualified for admission and were willing to prepare themselves, Pastor Hill and the congregation of Mount Zion Missionary Baptist Church would provide necessary financial support. To this day, when I return to that wonderful Christian fellowship, with him in the bosom of God, I publicly express my gratitude for their literal and emotional investment in my life and Christian ministry. My conscious ministerial acts (preaching, teaching, writing, and leading a thriving congregation) are returns on that investment.

The second manifestation I witnessed of a godly mentor's presence by way of provision was in the context of our denominational gathering. Again, as a kind father in the faith, Dr. Hill gathered at least eight of us and our wives for a meal in New Orleans. When the check came, he paid for the entire meal, to the tune of approximately $800! I learned an invaluable lesson that day, one that I vowed to implement myself as a "big-time" pastor one day.

Perhaps fifteen years later, after preaching before the National Baptist Convention in Orlando, Florida, I took ten members of our congregation who had come to share with me out to a fine Italian restaurant. And, you guessed it: I paid for the entire meal.

Lesson learned: being a spiritual father to others involves providing for them. Praise the Lord for the privilege!

7. **BLESS THE NEXT GENERATION**

I am saddened for my peers in Christian ministry, as many have never witnessed a true spiritual father in action, as the aforementioned examples illustrate his role. Not having witnessed it, they cannot articulate what it means to carry the title and responsibility of spiritual mentor to another, or to be mentored.

As I write, I am at a particularly fulfilling place in my own spiritual journey of Christian leadership. With more than thirty-seven years in ministry, thirty-two as a pastor, and yet my being in my mid-50s, I represent the in-between stage of Christian ministry. At the same time, I am honored by nearly ten men and women across America who affirm me as their spiritual father.

Just recently, a young pastor called my office. I did not know him, yet I took the call. He informed me of his name and church, and gave a bit of his background. We agreed to meet. He came to the office, sounding sincere in his faith and serious about God, with a willingness to learn. I told him that I had high standards for opening my heart, life, and resources to a young clergyman. If he was not truly committed to God, I informed him that he should tell me that at that time, as I did not have time to waste. Hearing all the right notes from him, I accepted his request. I sincerely pray that he will live up to God's high calling, fulfilling a grand purpose for life, leading the saints in Christ's mission, and advancing the kingdom of God through Jesus Christ, one soul at a time.

As I have been blessed by my spiritual mentors, I seek to impact the succeeding generation through significant emphases: the call of God, the call to prepare, reverence for God, prayerfulness, continual Bible study, discipline, integrity, excellence, character, professionalism, and compassion for people, while being supremely dedicated to the task.

8. EMOTIONAL GROUNDING

Simply stated, too many young clergy (in the age range of their twenties through their early forties) exhibit immaturity. While many are gifted communicators of the Word of God, some personal habits before congregants betray a lack of emotional grounding.

As I was taught by old-school mentors, I unwittingly have taken on their attitudes, appraisals, and actions.

The presence of a caring spiritual father, then, should mean helping younger leaders in the area of emotional grounding. Several ideas animate my thoughts, but I will confine them to two matters: dealing with challenges, and knowing what you stand for.

Any leader, especially a Christian one, will face challenges. The best way to deal with them is, of course, through prayer to God. In the practical sense, one must learn to gauge the severity of each challenge. It is astounding that the statement "I need to pray about this matter" will cause some spiritual storms to evaporate because it was, as one friend termed it, only a two-week issue—that is, after two weeks, no one would even notice it or talk about it. Things change so quickly! Today's headline will become tomorrow's old news.

What must become non-negotiable, however, for any Christian leader is one's core beliefs: salvation through Christ alone, by faith alone, by grace alone; the absolute authority of Scripture; the power of God's Holy Spirit; regular prayer to God; the reality of heaven, being eternally with the heavenly Father; the reality of hell, eternal separation from God because of rejecting Christ as Savior; the binding necessity of winning the unsaved to Christ; learning, interpreting, and applying all scriptural truth; seeing infinite potential in people as God does; relying upon the promises of God; and much more!

In closing, I admit bias: I had and still have spiritual fathers present in my life for whom I have deep respect and from whom I derive my understanding of the calling and work of Christian ministry, which should edify saints and advance the kingdom of God through Christ.

Therefore, I commend those today who are present in the lives of their spiritual sons and daughters in the Christian Gospel. Also, I challenge those who are not present: you will imperil those who need your godly input.

6

THE PRACTICES OF A SPIRITUAL FATHER
(PART I)

In the full exploration of all nuances of serving as a spiritual father to others, I have been animated by a persuasive concept: spiritual fathers acting in the name of Christ possess power to prompt younger Christian leaders toward big, bold, decisive, monumental, long-lasting achievements in the kingdom of God. Indeed, as father-mentors challenge son-protégés toward such an agenda, it will mean significant movement for Christendom in shaping a new paradigm for the twenty-first century.

Today, godly fathers should compel progeny in Christ to reach much higher than they achieved, no matter their stature in Christ. I am convinced that each generation should exceed the previous one, glorifying God, representing Christ, and advancing the kingdom of God while serving its particular epoch of human history. The baton of Christian faith must be intentionally passed on.

In another chapter of this book, I briefly mentioned how, as an impressionable clergy leader, I heard a stirring call by a wise denominational leader. He summoned African-American Baptists to join a multimillion-dollar capital campaign, which eventually led to the construction of our denominational headquarters, a stellar vision for a black Christian group. That episode thirty years ago remains fixed in my mind as a moment of spiritual clarity.

I was honored to share with thousands of other clergy and congregations in achieving something significant for the kingdom of God. Unfortunately, since that time, I have not heard another leader issue a feasible, tangible, compelling summons to something enduring for the Christian cause.

At various levels, I hear the small, narrow agendas of so-called leaders, especially miscalculating the impact of the body of Christ. Particularly, I am astounded that with black concerns at alarmingly high rates (unemployment, home-ownership/wealth deficits, college admission, corporate presence, poverty, family dysfunction, health care, domestic violence, absent fathers, incarceration, and pensions, among a few indices) there are not more black Christian leaders of national organizations raising their voices. Perhaps my trouble is expecting those with big microphones to be conversant with and compassionate toward the challenges parishioners face in daily living.

The dichotomy of "spiritual" versus "social" represents a false and unnecessary one, given that those in Christian pews need biblical, spiritual, and pragmatic principles for navigating this world. I advise leaders to affirm Christ as Savior and have a plan for fulsome engagement in the multifaceted issues of our day.

Currently, what pushes me as a middle-aged Christian leader emanates from hearing my father in the faith, the late Dr. Edward V. Hill of Los Angeles and global acclaim, pontificate on the important issues of his day from a prophetic perspective. A giant of the Christian faith, I recall his advising U.S. presidents, meeting with corporate titans, sharing in global efforts, speaking in national conferences, and making a tremendous difference for the kingdom of God. While never deviating from the Christ paradigm, Dr. Hill also focused on human suffering and tangible pain, offering real-world, personal responsibility solutions rather than victimization rhetoric. Watching these activities, first as a young leader and now by way of fond remembrance, I am still inspired by his worthy example.

Often in my consciousness, I hear a haunting refrain: "Attempt great things for God; expect great things from God." I learned that dictum from Dr. Hill, and it pushes me toward unusual exploits for the kingdom of God. I usually do not wait for permission from a clique to form my objectives. Instead, I reason that the majority may not be possessed of the faith-dynamic gene.

One of my brothers in Christ, having started Christian ministry alongside me under Dr. Hill's tutelage, now leads a strong pastorate in Washington, D.C. He facetiously says that he often teaches classes on "E. V. Hill Theology 101" to those ministers who were unable to meet the man in person.

Spiritual fathers, in my view, should promote among younger clergy several considerations: 1) unequivocal love for God; 2) continual prayer and worship; 3) adherence to the inspired, inerrant, infallible, authoritative Word of God; 4) recognition of the centrality of Christ; 5) reliance upon God's Holy Spirit; 6) fidelity to family and integrity; 7) commitment to reaching the lost; 8) teaching the saved fundamental principles of Christian discipleship; 9) the necessity of ongoing study and personal spiritual growth; 10) devotion to social justice; 11) articulation of big, unusual, out-of-the-box, novel, God-sized visions; 12) operations in the supernatural; and, 13) humility and accountability.

All of these ideals occur in the name of Christ, advancing God's kingdom. We shall briefly evaluate this baker's dozen of ideals from spiritual fathers. In Part I, we will discuss the first half of these father practices. In Part II, we will discuss the balance of these.

1. UNEQUIVOCAL LOVE FOR GOD

The surest way for a father in the faith to shape the next generation of spiritual leadership in the Christian faith community is by expressing and modeling a life totally transformed by an unequivocal love for God. Spiritual fathers greatly impact those under their spiritual care, particularly younger ministers, by driving home a central fact: "I really love God, and by Him all things in my life have been made possible." My personal reference point was hearing a riveting account of the spiritual conversion of a pastor who told me what God in Christ had done for him, along with what He could do for me. In reality, my walk with God has been directly shaped by wanting to love God in the simple yet profound manner that my spiritual leader embraced Him.

More than empty religiosity, suggestive of some remote, absent, unfathomable, disconnected, amorphous, "power within," I was introduced to the gracious, merciful, compassionate, alive, alert, engaged heavenly Father. That same heavenly Father created the world and governs it as well, taking notice of me. In His ultimate act of grace, that same Father sent His only Son to reconcile me in righteousness, not through what I could do to merit salvation, but in what His Son achieved on my behalf. Note how the Word characterizes, crystallizes, and catalogues this profound truth: "By this the love of God was manifested in us, that God has sent His only begotten Son into the world so that we might live through Him. In this is love, not that we loved God, but that He loved us and sent His Son to be the propitiation for our sins" (1 John 4:9-10).

Daily, then, I thank God for those influences, after my own mother, who taught me to passionately love God. The God I know intimately through Christ serves as the only explanation for anything of substance that I celebrate. And I live within the context of an embedded principle: "My love for God is predicated on the love of God." Indeed, I constantly reflect on God who first loved me, and loves me still, though I habitually fall short of that love.

During times of stress, struggle, and strain, seeking to share the sense of where God wants to take our congregation, the love of God propels me onward. Perhaps it will strike some as simplistic, but my pastor convinced me both that God loved me and, critically, I could in turn love Him.

2. CONTINUAL PRAYER AND WORSHIP

A further benefit from a spiritual father involves inculcation of prayerfulness and worship in younger clergy. Incredibly, I am convinced that some Christians, even clergy, tire of prayer. Yet, prayer brings saints into intimacy with God. The Word confirms it: "Pray without ceasing" (1 Thessalonians 5:17). Concomitantly, saints exist to worship God! I have never engaged in the "Christians don't have to go to church to be saved" conversation. Instead, I have wondered, "Why would I want to intentionally stay away from the sanctuary, sanctified for the purpose of honoring the God of creation and salvation, gathering with other saints in the name of His Son, Jesus?" In that spirit, then, I am unalterably a worshipper.

Over the course of my first fifty-four years of life, I can count the times I have not been in the assembly of the righteous in worship in the name of Jesus on a given Sunday morning. Going to worship seems, to me, as normative as breathing. Regularly, and with relish, I do it to live!

I am eternally grateful for spiritual leaders who taught me the critical value of coming before God as a worshipper. They taught and modeled the Scriptures: "Come, let us worship and bow down, Let us kneel before the LORD our Maker" (Psalm 95:6); and, "Not to us, O LORD, not to us, But to Your name give glory" (Psalm 115:1a); and, "I was glad when they said to me, 'Let us go to the house of the LORD'" (Psalm 122:1); and, "But an hour is coming, and now is, when the true worshippers will worship the Father in spirit and truth; for such people the Father seeks to be His worshipers. God is spirit, and those who worship Him must worship in spirit and truth" (John 4:23-24); and, "Not forsaking our own assembling together, as is the habit of some, but encouraging one another; and all the more as you see the day drawing near" (Hebrews 10:25).

So, worship-themed Scriptures establish my spiritual foundation. Upon those bases, God has built a long-time Christian faith and a national Christian ministry. Worship of God celebrates regular, spirited time in His powerful presence, honoring Him both for who He is and for all He does. True worship revolves around a glorious, awesome, wonderful God! This I learned from men and women of considerable faith in God. Worship and praise from central planks in my existence. The contemporary praise maestro Pastor William Murphy captures it well:

> *Praise is what I do, when I want to be close to You.*
> *I lift my hands in praise.*
> *Praise is who I am.*
> *I will praise Him while I can.*
> *I'll bless Him at all times.*
>
> *I vow to praise You,*
> *Through the good and the bad,*
> *I'll praise You,*
> *Whether happy or sad.*
> *I'll praise You,*
> *In all that I go through,*
> *Because praise is what I do,*
> *Cause I owe it all to You.*
> *Praise is what I do,*
>
> *Even when I am going through,*
> *See, I want to let the devil know, tonight,*
> *Though my circumstance doesn't even stand a chance,*
> *My praise outweighs the bad.*

While writing these words, I have had to pause to praise the Lord!

Murphy taps into something transcendent: those who love God, insistent on worship of Him, must never allow fleeting circumstances—job loss, illness, relational failure, bankruptcy, pain, challenge, or whatever—to dictate their response to God. We worship Him despite it all!

3. ADHERENCE TO THE INSPIRED, INERRANT, INFALLIBLE, AUTHORITATIVE WORD OF GOD

Ministerial success in Christianity will be engendered by adherence to the biblical standard above any other source of information. God's Word has successfully weathered every test by any scoffer, skeptic, or cynical observer. Accordingly, we really need obsessive fathers in the faith who hold that God's Word settles every matter pertaining to faith and practice. Today, I fear many clergy—and by extension Christian congregations—genuflect before the altar of expedience, seeking secular ways to attract people. In the process, they compromise orthodox truth, diluting it with pop culture, psychology, mysticism, and inspirational and motivational jargon. The cumulative effect forsakes the power of the unadulterated biblical message centered in Jesus Christ.

While aiming to remain relevant through technology, maintaining an accurate read on the human condition, I vow to remain wed to an orthodox, biblical, Christ-exalting tradition over anything else. Perhaps it is my vivid imagination, but I hear some mentors asking, "Collier, what is this new stuff you fellows are preaching?" In response, I say, "It is as bothersome to me as to you; please tell the perpetrators of your concerns."

More than commentaries, newspapers, periodicals, scholarly journals, Internet blogs, influential books, or other sources, Christian ministers must be unalterably riveted to the biblical record: "All Scripture is inspired by God and profitable for teaching, for reproof, for correction, for training in righteousness; so that the man of God may be adequate, equipped for every good work" (2 Timothy 3:16-17). Interestingly, these words were originally given by a spiritual mentor, Paul, to his beloved protégé Timothy. Paul offered the words for the wider benefit of those saints of God who would come under Timothy's spiritual care. Indeed, God's people receive spiritual nurture through intake and application of the inspired, inerrant, infallible, unassailable, authoritative Word of God.

The danger in a Christian leader's making too many references to cultural touchstones (movies, music, infamous celebrities, and trends) is that these may compete with the inspired, infallible, authoritative Word of God. Let me state it clearly: every sincere Gospel preacher should proclaim the Word of God. Cultural references should represent, at best, illustrations of a central biblical principle. The principle, then, must be applied to everyday living if congregants and visitors are to receive benefits.

Thank God for dogmatic spiritual fathers who would not relent in holding me to the sure underpinnings of the Word of God, applying its seminal principles. I am richer and a better servant-leader, along with innumerable congregants, due to their insistence. Cultural references fade, but the Word of God remains forever!

4. RECOGNITION OF THE CENTRALITY OF CHRIST

Christians should also appreciate caring spiritual patrons who talked incessantly of the centrality of Christ—for access to God, eternal life, ongoing faith, answered prayers, and, truly, the entirety of Christian life. These mentors are special gifts from God. Through pre-figuring in the Old Testament, extending to His advent in the New, Christ embodies God's ultimate extension of grace to humanity: "And the Word became flesh, and dwelt among us, and we saw His glory, glory as of the only begotten from the Father, full of grace and truth" (John 1:14).

I am extremely grateful for godly mentors' calling me to salvation through the risen Savior: "And there is salvation in no one else; for there is no other name under heaven that has been given among men by which we must be saved" (Acts 4:12). That bedrock spiritual principle has stood the ravages of time, ensuring that salvation rests on what God did for humanity in Christ, rather than on any of humanity's meritorious achievements.

Clad in clerical vestments or black suits, my mentors in the Christian faith within the African-American Baptist tradition were convinced that preaching was incomplete unless or until one "went to the Cross." For them (and me), Christ's work of fostering salvation for humanity culminated in God's raising Christ from the dead, "early Sunday morning." While human psychology and theological training have embellished depth, insight, and nuance of that resurrection truth, adding a wide vocabulary and metaphysical concepts, it has not in any way altered its necessity. After all is said, everything in the spiritual realm revolves around Christ. Real life begins at a place called Calvary.

As strong, clear, dynamic, passionate proclamation of the Gospel of Christ (His life, death, burial, resurrection, ascension, and imminent return) goes forth in American congregations, it will foster their resurgence. The Christian message of forgiveness, liberation, hope, and purpose will serve so many who are unsaved and living beneath God's standard.

Today, we dare not equate Christ—in the name of religious tolerance, diversity of opinion, or respect for other faith traditions—with any other historic figure. Christ alone retains power to draw humanity to God: "that God was in Christ reconciling the world to Himself, not counting their trespasses against them. . . . He made Him who knew no sin to be sin on our behalf, so that we might become the righteousness of God in Him" (2 Corinthians 5:19a, 21). Faced with the tremendous significance God placed on Christ, affirming His passion for humanity, we must not trivialize Him in contemporary preaching, teaching, or living.

Christ is not a religious leader on par with Muhammad or Abraham, making Islam, Judaism, and Christianity three viable options in coming to God. Rather, Christ alone enables a relationship with the heavenly Father: "I am the way, and the truth, and the life; no one comes to the Father but through Me" (John 14:6).

Spiritual fathers of yesteryear sacrificed themselves for the centrality of Christ. They were fully persuaded of His sufficiency, substance, and saving power for all humanity. In light of that Christ-oriented legacy, Christian leaders today owe their mentors. Younger clergy should, as with a relay baton, pass the same truth on to succeeding generations.

5. RELIANCE UPON GOD'S HOLY SPIRIT

Christianity was never meant to be lived, nor can maturity be achieved apart from reliance upon the indwelling presence of God's Holy Spirit in the believer. Again, I salute and celebrate spiritual fathers for implanting that revelation from God in my mind, heart, and spirit. Indeed, I heard about "unction," "anointing," and "endowment" well before I fully captured their essence in Scripture.

These mentors validated the Scriptures: "'Not by might nor by power, but by My Spirit,' says the LORD of hosts" (Zechariah 4:6b); and, "I will ask the Father, and He will give you another Helper, that He may be with you forever; that is the Spirit of truth, whom the world cannot receive, because it does not see Him or know Him, but you know Him because He abides with you and will be in you. . . . But the Helper, the Holy Spirit, whom the Father will send in My name, He will teach you all things, and bring to your remembrance all that I said to you" (John 14:16-17, 26).

With my appetite whet by the fathers' multiple references to the Holy Spirit, prompted by God's Holy Spirit, I plunged deeper into biblical study. There I came to understand additional applications of His influence among yielded Christians: "You were sealed in Him with the Holy Spirit of promise, who is given as a pledge of our inheritance, with a view to the redemption of God's own possession, to the praise of His glory" (Ephesians 1:13b-14).

Within the context of preaching "the whole counsel of God," I was better than blessed in hearing spiritual fathers tell of all that God would do for me as a saint of God as I relied upon His Holy Spirit for the forward direction of my life.

As I reflect on what now seems like the golden age (1960s to 1990s) of Christian engagement, it was as though these fathers in the faith were intentionally aiming for depth of biblical knowledge. Even if they were not seminary trained, they studiously explored and researched the Word. In the process, God's Holy Spirit revealed more to them than some esteemed theological professors could express.

Today, standing upon the broad shoulders of fathers in glory, I embrace deeper teaching relative to personality, deity, convicting, regenerating, baptizing, filling, illumination, gifts, fruit, guiding, and other aspects of God's Holy Spirit. (While too many in the body of Christ fight over the meaning of the Spirit's work, none can deny that He must work!) Younger clergy, then, in my view, must totally rely upon God's Holy Spirit. Accordingly, we need Him while rejecting gimmicks, charisma, wit, erudition, scheming, or any other human ploy.

6. FIDELITY TO FAMILY AND INTEGRITY

While blessed to observe a few spiritual fathers quite closely, I noted the high premium they placed on their families. As proud black men, they fiercely carved out emotional territory for wives and children. Moreover, they wanted to provide for their families' needs. Of course, in some cases, zeal for serving God's people caused some to miss football games, track meets, cheerleading events, recitals, and the like. In their absence, PKs (preacher's kids) very well may have harbored resentments, knowing that if not for congregational duties, their fathers would have been present. At the 2003 memorial of my pastor, Dr. Edward V. Hill, I thanked his children for lending him to so many of us, helping us to become better young people and adults.

In a survey of distinguished spiritual fathers, the "godfather" of black Chicago, Dr. Clay Evans, said that he was the most proud of having experienced fifty-plus years of marriage to his beloved wife. He listed his marriage above leading a great church; above recording gospel albums; above mentoring great preachers; above preaching revivals; and above acclaim afforded by decades in Christian ministry.

Further, these godly fathers, though imperfect, were vivid examples of marital commitment in an American culture too often given to immorality, disposability, and indifference to personal integrity. In the majority of cases I witnessed, they handled sensitive matters with utter discretion, making their ministries, their marriages, and their money sacrosanct.

Godly fathers of an earlier generation knew well the Scripture: "For we do not preach ourselves but Christ Jesus as Lord, and ourselves as your bond-servants for Jesus' sake. . . . But we have this treasure in earthen vessels, so that the surpassing greatness of the power will be of God and not from ourselves" (2 Corinthians 4:5, 7).

From these spiritual leaders, then, I heard the quote from John: "He must increase, but I must decrease" (John 3:30). In so many ways, they practiced integrity of profession without viewing themselves as secular professionals. Like John the Baptizer, their self-assessment was clear: "'I am a VOICE OF ONE CRYING IN THE WILDERNESS, "MAKE STRAIGHT THE WAY OF THE LORD"'" (John 1:23).

Moreover, personal integrity characterized the majority of spiritual fathers. The ones I admired and emulated were steadfast in giving their word as to where they stood, while expecting the same from others. Today, I am sad to report, in too many cases we lack the same level of integrity, especially among clergy. Perhaps in the mad rush of life too many overschedule and overextend themselves, resulting in failure to honor commitments, large and small. When a man fails to return a phone call, a text, a fax, a letter, or some other means of communication in a timely manner, it bespeaks his integrity, or lack thereof. His title in Christian ministry does not matter; he forsakes the mantle of integrity —period!

These practices by the spiritual fathers (along with more to follow in the next chapter) were foundational for transmitting a body of knowledge and experiences for a successful Christian ministry for the long haul. The whole notion of their work sought to advance the kingdom of God through Jesus Christ.

The best metaphor for these godly father practices involves a collection of intellectual archives to which younger clergy may turn for a lifetime of responses to current and emerging concerns of the body of Christ, along with all who will be persuaded to make Christ their Savior and Lord.

Read on for further critical practices.

7

THE PRACTICES OF A SPIRITUAL FATHER
(PART II)

As the Christian witness takes inventory of its blessings, one main benefit is the body of practices passed from spiritual fathers to their progeny. In the previous chapter, we celebrated several principles and practices for the advancing of the kingdom of God through Jesus Christ.

In this chapter, we will add to and amplify these practices (continuing from #6 in the previous chapter).

7. COMMITMENT TO REACHING THE UNSAVED

A further reason I relish my spiritual fathers is that they were adamant regarding reaching the skeptic, the unsaved, and the unchurched. They pushed Christian saints, congregations, and ecclesiological groups to remember Christ's mission of making disciples (see Matthew 28:19). The fathers I hold in the highest esteem knew that millions in America were lost because they had failed to ask Christ to become their Savior and Lord.

Like drill sergeants in the military, these fathers were constantly gauging ministry effectiveness according to conversions, baptisms, additions, and restorations to faithfulness. More than aiming at members to come to church, they searched for those ready to, instead, come to Christ. More than gaining a "lost coin," they yearned for "lost sheep" (see Luke 15). That sentiment today should still represent the objective of the Christian witness. Soul winning for Christ yet remains the distinctive mission of the twenty-first-century Christian church.

As envisioned by spiritual fathers, weeklong crusades were intended to lead persons to salvation through Christ. Anointed, gifted ministers, those known for Gospel-preaching prowess, were invited to share the Word, hoping to ignite a fire of evangelistic enthusiasm. Uncles, cousins, brothers, nephews, sisters, aunts, nieces, neighbors, friends, co-workers, and strangers were brought together in prayer, amid singing influenced by God's Holy Spirit, with Christ at the summit—while joyful possibilities abounded.

The resurgence of Christianity as a dominant force in American life depends in no small measure on its embracing evangelism. Evangelical enthusiasm must once again become the foremost calling of everyone who knows what Christ does for every life: He makes persons new. Thereafter, they rejoice in forgiveness from the heavenly Father, a fresh focus in righteousness, an outlook toward the possibilities of their future, and a perspective allowing them to see God as Protector and Provider, rather than as a menacing foe.

All spiritual fathers—some reaching retirement age, while some seek to burnish their leadership legacies—must accept that Christian evangelism possesses singular power to radically transform the landscape of the Christian witness. Intentional evangelism reminds all saints of Christ's mission of advancing the kingdom of God in this world. What excites me in this critical hour in the life of the Lord's church is the degree to which Christian leaders can positively impact the trajectory of our focus. If preaching, teaching, and programming in local Christian fellowships take the deliberate route of evangelizing the unsaved, it will lead to new converts. Such persons will bring questions, ideas, notions, and concepts, all which will lead to renewed energy and dynamism for the body of Christ.

8. TEACHING THE SAVED FUNDAMENTAL PRINCIPLES OF CHRISTIAN DISCIPLESHIP

I regularly encounter Christians who fondly recall spiritual fathers who taught them regarding what would produce Christian growth, while fostering deeper discipleship. They reference men who were prayer warriors, calling down fire, similar to the prophet Elijah in the Old Testament. They extol the exploits of men who took pennies, nickels, and dimes in the African-American faith tradition, using those meager means to establish multiple outreaches (building sanctuaries, renovating properties, supporting foreign missions, feeding the needy, using the medium of radio/television, opening daycares, Christian schools, youth programs, job training, and more).

In earlier generations, something prosaic as Sunday school, training periods, or evening worship were indispensable, conveying biblical principles for Christian discipleship. Often in times past, the Sunday schedule was jam-packed with times in the sanctuary; yet it helped those who applied themselves to get deeper into the Word of God. Of course, the quantity of Christian gatherings could not guarantee the quality of a saint's walk with God. But the likelihood increased of one's coming to know more about Christ because of frequent encounters with dedicated, intensive study of the Scriptures. Some of the godly fathers, to their credit, captured the relevant Word: "So faith comes from hearing, and hearing by the word of Christ" (Romans 10:17). Not surprisingly, these wise leaders championed a paradigm of steady intake of the Word as foundational for Christian growth: "Like newborn babies, long for the pure milk of the word, so that by it you may grow in respect to salvation, if you have tasted the kindness of the Lord" (1 Peter 2:2-3).

When many reflect, they are astounded as to how much time they devoted to church activities, especially in comparison to how today many want to grow in Christ, yet they often subsist on one, short worship period on Sundays without spending time in corporate Bible study or ministry gatherings throughout the week. I have heard sincere Christians argue that life today is more hectic, as if we still do not have twenty-four hours in a given day, or seven days in a given week.

I believe a subtle attack of the enemy is to bombard Christians with a mountain of benign activities (television, entertainment, sports, dating, going to the gym, times enjoying family and friends), which crowd out time for immersion in the things of God (Bible study, prayer, fasting, small-group discipleship, attending weekly ministry meetings). Lacking such spiritual grounding, many wonder why they are fatigued, stressed, frustrated, and empty.

Perhaps I must state it plainly: Christian discipleship will never emerge from listening to great sermons, watching great leaders, attending large churches, going to Christian conferences, or fellowshipping with other saints. No—Christian growth leading to real discipleship emanates from going deeper into the wonders of prayer, while extracting principles from the Word of God. These principles must be fully understood, faithfully applied, and fervently practiced.

When we marvel at the athletic abilities of our favorite professional athletes in any sport, we should recognize the countless hours spent honing his/her craft. Similarly, if we expect continuing manifestations of maturity and discipleship, they will come through our putting in "reps" in worship, prayer, obedience, sharing the faith, tithing, and practicing holiness before the Lord. Indeed, lasting godliness results from arduous, rigorous, continual training.

The spiritual fathers, praise the Lord, provided the template for discipleship. The question lingers, "Did we really catch their focus on developing in discipleship?" If we did, it will be seen in our current devotion to all they taught. The best barometer of whether one received such teaching is not repeating their sayings, or nostalgia; but we honor them and what they taught through ongoing dedication to biblical principles. Teachers may teach, but students must learn if the education loop is to prove successful.

9. NECESSITY OF ONGOING STUDY AND PERSONAL SPIRITUAL ENRICHMENT

A connected concept holds that many spiritual fathers distinguish themselves as lifelong learners. I recall many with intense curiosity well into their eighties. I recall many with a new book in their hands. I recall many asking questions of young seminarians, debating hot topics of the day. Despite their advanced years, the fathers still recognized their opportunity to shape the course of world events, especially from a Christian perspective. Of course, personal pride would not allow most to express that there was much that younger clergy could teach them.

Nevertheless, it has been noteworthy that new methods have been adopted by old-school godly fathers! I smile as I note seventy-year-old preachers preaching from iPads, or leading Bible study using PowerPoint. Many fathers twenty years my senior navigate technology better than I! This represents an instance of technology being put to good use, bringing glory to God.

The dynamic between spiritual fathers' wisdom and spiritual sons' technological savvy, for example, represents a great model for Christian engagement. Mentors enjoy the spirited back-and-forth achieved when their ideas, expertise, and exposure are celebrated, while opening themselves to contemporary jargon, notions, and trends as long as they respect foundations of biblical, spiritual, relational, cultural, and practical truth, all centering in Jesus Christ.

On the other hand, insightful protégés should enjoy the anecdotes, reflections, and gravitas of fathers, taking advantage of hard-earned insight without all the heartaches. A mentor exposes a protégé to the mentor's body of knowledge so that the protégé can bypass the pain of the process.

An Old Testament episode reminds us of the yearning for engagement by the elderly warrior Caleb. His ambition, undiminished by advanced years, was remarkable:

> "Now behold, the LORD has let me live, just as He spoke, these forty-five years, from the time that the LORD spoke this word to Moses, when Israel walked in the wilderness; and now behold, I am eighty-five years old today. I am still as strong today as I was in the day Moses sent me; as my strength was then, so my strength is now, for war and for going out and coming in. Now then, give me this hill country . . ." (Joshua 14:10-12)

Therefore, spiritual fathers motivate succeeding generations of saints by their unbridled zeal for God, for His glory, and for taking new territory in the faith dimension.

Even if we concede that Caleb may have been overly ambitious, with more desire than ability, we must agree that his challenge to Joshua and others around him electrified those prone to give less than their best in service to God, retreating in the face of adversity. Conquering the Promised Land then, as does living for God now, required/requires faith, focus, and fortitude, among many other traits. Strong spiritual fathers produce strength and resilience in their progeny. Notice in the above-quoted verse the number of times Caleb referenced "strength." Today represents the absolute wrong time to exhibit weakness of character or uncertainty. Instead, we need godly fathers to challenge Christians to the "last measure" of fight within!

Indeed, I am deeply moved when an elder statesman of the Christian pulpit says, "Collier, I have been thinking about . . . ." It signals to me that the Caleb spirit is alive and well in him. Endowed wisdom yearns for places to share it, and that for the benefit of the next generation of Christian leaders and congregants.

Now, a father may have informed me as to his thoughts so as to engage me in the implementation of those plans. If so, I am ready for the "fight," if aided by his wise counsel. That is what I envision and what underpins this book: spiritual fathers and spiritual sons yoked in battle, leading the forces of Christ, advancing the kingdom of God.

When Christian leaders cease to learn (wide reading, meditation, conferences, discussions, active dreaming), all those under their spiritual influence are left to acquire principles for discipleship by their own devices. The result, most often fragmented, chaotic, and catastrophic in its implications, both now, and into the future, will hamper millions of saints. Conversely, rich principles of Christian discipleship will bolster the faith of equals of millions.

10. DEVOTION TO SOCIAL JUSTICE

During a particularly violent period in my native Los Angeles, a group of ministers led by a few spiritual fathers went, without appointment, to the L.A. mayor's office. We demanded that the mayor direct the police chief to deploy more officers to a very dangerous area. In the name of social justice, we were acting as Christian leaders to save the lives of young people as the mix of gang culture and drug sales threatened to devastate low-income black communities.

Later, in 1992, in the aftermath of the L.A. riots, spiritual fathers came together to discuss and tackle the challenges of neglected communities, which had provided "fuel" for incendiary proclivities. When then-president George H. W. Bush came to south Los Angeles after the riots, he was received by godly fathers, men of faith, and a watching community. Critically, President Bush spoke in a black church setting (Mount Zion Baptist Church, Los Angeles, whose pastor was Dr. E. V. Hill).

I cite these two examples of engagement by spiritual fathers because they accentuate their roles as shapers of community consensus. Beyond the needs of their own congregations, these men set a paradigm for spiritual leadership in a broader sense. As an eyewitness and younger participant in these efforts, I saw what God could do through yielded instruments, raising issues of concern for people without a voice. Some in communities know that brutality, indignity, suffering, and neglect occur; they simply cannot fully articulate what needs to be done. In that vacuum is where a dynamic, anointed, informed, spiritual leader—young or old—must operate.

This social-justice model is progressively prophetic and based in Scripture: "But let justice roll down like waters And righteousness like an ever-flowing stream" (Amos 5:24); or, "Cry loudly, do not hold back; Raise your voice like a trumpet, And declare to My people their transgression And to the house of Jacob their sins." . . . "Those from among you will rebuild the ancient ruins; You will raise up the age-old foundations; And you will be called the repairer of the breach, The restorer of the streets in which to dwell" (Isaiah 58:1, 12); or, "He has told you, O man, what is good; And what does the LORD require of you But to do justice, to love kindness, And to walk humbly with your God?" (Micah 6:8).

Today, the social-justice motif means that spiritual leaders must be very concerned with ample employment, education, housing, health care, help for ex-felons, public safety, and recreation for all families and individuals irrespective of race, ethnicity, gender, locale, orientation, or class. That, in my view, represents holistic ministry in the name of Christ.

11. ARTICULATION OF A GOD-SIZED VISION

Proper respect and gratitude should be directed to godly mentors who continually promote(d) a fresh, compelling, well-articulated vision from God. These fathers knew that a strong vision from God would directly and indirectly impact those falling under the shadow of their leadership. Being risk-averse, the fathers in the faith knew that, despite the immensity of the challenge, God met persons of unusual faith and determination. As a youth, then serving as a very young pastor myself, I witnessed men share their vision for a congregation. Often, the response was incredulity: too high a cost, and too remote its realization. Indeed, in the criticism lay recognition that if this vision was to prove successful, God must do it!

"It will come about after this That I will pour out My spirit on all mankind; And your sons and daughters will prophesy, Your old men will dream dreams, Your young men will see visions" (Joel 2:28). This prophecy represents God's description of spiritual progression. It validates both the mentor and protégé. Old men may revert to nostalgia ("dream dreams"), while young men express grand designs for the future ("see visions"). Significant achievement in one generation will be succeeded by similar exploits in the next one.

I was inspired then, and am moved still, by fathers in the faith articulating a large, substantive, unusual, Christ-affirming, people-based vision that enhances the kingdom of God. When the words *impossible* and *outlandish* were applied to it, I sensed the necessity of God in bringing such a vision to fruition. Count me in support of such a vision. I know that only visions befitting God's honor are large, complicated, timely, and timeless. Today, then, I implore Christian leaders: pray for and diligently seek an outsized vision from God.

12. OPERATIONS IN THE SUPERNATURAL

Closely related, I celebrate spiritual fathers who were clear in their mission: operating in the supernatural. They were venturing into territory marked off by God. It was fraught with danger, doubt, and disturbances. Note the Word: "For our struggle is not against flesh and blood, but against the rulers, against the powers, against the world forces of this darkness, against the spiritual forces of wickedness in the heavenly places" (Ephesians 6:12).

Often in Christian ministry today, it seems Christian leaders and parishioners forget that we are engaged in a fever-pitched battle with the enemy that hopes to nullify the advance of the kingdom of God by keeping lost souls blinded from the truth. Satan and his minions seek to prevent humanity from enjoying the full benefits of reconciliation with the heavenly Father through Christ. On the other hand, God wants His own to reach out to the unsaved with the truth of His unconditional love. Unfortunately, that message is too often muddled, allowing satanic devices to flourish, resulting in wasted lives.

Because of the supernatural nature of Christianity, we pray, we fast, we study the Word, we share our faith, we obey God, we confront the adversary in the name of Jesus, and we plead the blood of Jesus, expecting stupendous results in every God-or-dained, Christ-exalting, Spirit-led, kingdom-expanding venture! As saints of God, redeemed in Christ, emboldened by God's Word, and resolute in faith, we truly expect to overcome, while bringing others to salvation, hope, confidence, and advancement. Made alive in and by Christ, in every endeavor our origin is divine, our purpose redemptive, our personnel diverse, and our operation supernatural. We live by this biblical credo: "'No weapon that is formed against you will prosper; And every tongue that accuses you in judgment you will condemn. This is the heritage of the servants of the LORD, And their vindication is from Me,' declares the LORD" (Isaiah 54:17); and, "This is the LORD's doing; It is marvelous in our eyes. This is the day which the LORD has made; Let us rejoice and be glad in it" (Psalm 118:23-24).

From spiritual fathers, then, current saints learn of their spiritual lineage from God through Christ, lifting us to unknown heights. Thus, we bask in the wonders of the supernatural: "Now to Him who is able to do far more abundantly beyond all that we ask or think, according to the power that works within us, to Him be the glory in the church and in Christ Jesus to all generations forever and ever. Amen" (Ephesians 3:20-21).

13. HUMILITY AND ACCOUNTABILITY

The sublime lesson falling from spiritual fathers I observed was one of applying humility to every facet of Christian ministry.

Affirming God's call to service as His gracious choice rather than a nod to a meritorious individual, one father said it well: "Preachers should wear humility on their shirt sleeves, adorned with cufflinks of gratitude." The Bible sums it up even better: "Humble yourselves under the mighty hand of God, that He may exalt you at the proper time" (1 Peter 5:6). Note three significant facts: 1) we humble ourselves; 2) God's "mighty hand" represents multiple ways of humbling us; and, 3) at the proper time, such humility leads to exaltation by God.

As a result, as Christian leaders we must always bear in my mind our accountability to the heavenly Father. Despite acclaim, applause, adulation, and all metrics of a successful ministry, at the end the question from God will be, "Son, what did you do with all the gifts I gave to you?" In that moment, we shall recognize accountability before the One who gave us life, family, health, a voice, limitless opportunities, friends, placement, favor, and so much more.

Christian practices are spurred by Christian principles. Spiritual fathers of old were adamant regarding core biblical and doctrinal truths to which they continually turned, giving their ministries heft, anointing, substance, and longevity. If current Christian leaders, present parishioners, and those coming to the Christian faith put their minds on these practices, there is no limit to their benefit to the Master's kingdom cause.

Nothing changes for the Christian church unless and until more leaders realize the core of Christian concerns. Then, they should put the afore-stated practices into effect.

8

THE PROTECTION OF A SPIRITUAL FATHER

Perhaps it is impossible to fully convey the sense of security and safety involved in a healthy, nurturing, godly relationship with an enlightened and engaged spiritual father. Like many things, one either experiences it or one does not. Surely, for most Christian clergy that protection starts early in Christian ministry and continues throughout. Mentor and protégé have a formidable bond in Jesus Christ. Therefore, let us examine the contours of protection afforded by a spiritual father in various dimensions, starting from the inception of ministry, the divine call from the heavenly Father.

When God starts a Christian leader on a path of impacting others for the advancement of God's kingdom in Christ, it is a monumental endeavor. The treasure of the Gospel message within that individual must be protected from the beginning until the end. Such a person becomes the instrument through which God will share messages of hope, forgiveness, and grace to thousands over a life of Christian dedication. So it is imperative that the right spiritual father connects with the one who will transmit the Good News of Christ that transforms lives. From the first day, this prototypical spiritual mentor starts shaping his protégé for the work ahead, serving as a protective patron and partner.

I trust you will indulge me as I explain the divine calling to Christian ministry within the context of biblical narratives. Then I will share the multiple blessings of being under the protective care of spiritual fathers who guided me in a fundamental undertaking. That undertaking, though nearly four decades old, has continually shaped my identity, mission, fulfillment, and destiny in the kingdom of God.

When an individual in right relationship with God, through saving faith in the Lord, Jesus Christ, comes to the full realization of a divine call upon his/her life, the first reaction should be sincere humility before God. None should approach Christian ministry separate from a specific call from God. Far greater than a commitment to the "family business" (son or daughter of a minister), feeling suited to helping others, or a means of social engagement (a sociology major), Christian ministry operates from the premise that God makes a special selection of an individual for service to Him.

Critically, God's choice of those who are to proclaim His Word and serve His people involves a gracious act on His part, not a badge of merit for the called. Indeed, God "qualifies the called" rather than "calling the qualified."

Dr. William Pannell, "father of black evangelicalism" and trailblazing African-American scholar at my alma mater, Fuller Theological Seminary, put the call from God in this language: "That verse of Scripture (Ephesians 1) jumped out, grabbed me by the throat, wrapped itself around my heart, and I'm telling you, I've never gotten over it. Here was this young, green-as-grass, African-American kid, in a kind of genteel segregated town. And there was the God of eternity marking this kid off for Himself, putting a call on him: "You're mine.' You don't get over that!" (*Fuller Magazine*, Issue 1, 2014, p. 21).

Note the apostle Paul's interpretation of God's call upon his life:

I thank Christ Jesus our Lord, who has strengthened me, because He considered me faithful, putting me into service;

even though I was formerly a blasphemer and a persecutor and a violent aggressor. Yet I was shown mercy because I acted ignorantly in unbelief; and the grace of our Lord was more than abundant, with the faith and love which are found in Christ Jesus. . . . Yet for this reason I found mercy, so that in me as the foremost, Jesus Christ might demonstrate His perfect patience as an example for those who would believe in Him for eternal life. (1 Timothy 1:12-14, 16)

In my mind, it is remarkable that Paul, God's stellar instrument in advancing His kingdom through Jesus Christ, aside from the Savior Himself, would evaluate himself as the "foremost" sinner. I, for one, would argue with that characterization, for over my years of preaching, teaching, counseling, and leading God's people, I still feel inadequate, ill-prepared, and unworthy of this high, supernatural, divine calling! (I keep reminding God that in me He chose a fundamentally flawed, flailing, sometimes fearful, yet faithful, fixated servant.) So I persist in ministry to the glory of the Father, for the lifting of His Son, by the power of His Spirit.

If one is specifically convinced of a divine call to ministry, one should immediately go into serious prayer, asking God for clear answers: *Heavenly Father, is this Your perfect will for my life? Did I hear You clearly, as to my spiritual destiny? Reveal to me the substance of Your calling. Please purify me of any sense of self-reliance or self-aggrandizement. Humbly, I ask that You guide me through this undertaking. Allow me to appreciate Your glorious hand in my life. Work through me, a yielded vessel, for the proclamation of Your Word. Let others come to saving faith in Your Son. Anoint me in the power of Your Holy Spirit. I submit this petition to You, in the name of Jesus. Amen.*

Of course, the prayer will vary from person to person; yet, it will coincide with the nature of one's relationship with God. More than the words—one must take this life-altering matter before the throne of grace. While God will answer in ways consistent with His sovereign will as reflected in the biblical record, He will reveal the divine plan for every would-be servant.

Relative to the divine call, in African-American preaching lore, there are ministers who were "sent," along with others who "just went." Through prayer and sincerity, one must ensure being in the former category rather than in the latter one. In dire and difficult moments, some can only rely upon, "Lord, I know You called me to this. So I will continue on. Please help me."

From the biblical record, we develop a sense of the various methods by which God specifically called those He intended to use: "When the LORD saw that [Moses] turned aside to look, God called to him from the midst of the bush and said, 'Moses, Moses!' And he said, 'Here I am'" (Exodus 3:4). Scholars refer to this and other thrilling episodes as "call narratives" in Scripture. They seek to capture the weight of divine intervention in specific lives: patriarchs, prophets, and preachers.

In the Old Testament, another riveting call narrative featured the young man Samuel: "So the LORD called Samuel again for the third time. And he arose and went to Eli and said, 'Here I am, for you called me.' Then Eli discerned that the LORD was calling the boy" (1 Samuel 3:8). Indeed, these call narratives become quite instructional, as they reveal God's clear intention to place specific persons in lifetime employ for the achievement of the divine plan and for His greater glory.

Because of the nature of the undertaking—sharing redemptive truth with alienated humanity—service for God represents a definitive divine call from heaven: "Then I heard the voice of the LORD, saying, 'Whom shall I send, and who will go for Us?'" (Isaiah 6:8); and, "Before I formed you in the womb I knew you, And before you were born I consecrated you; I have appointed you a prophet to the nations" (Jeremiah 1:5).

By the New Testament, highlighting the coming of the Son of God, Jesus Christ, as the Savior of the world, we note the continuation of God's purpose, enlisting individuals in His plan, starting with a beloved messenger: "you will give him the name John. . . .

and many will rejoice at his birth . . . and he will be filled with the Holy Spirit while yet in his mother's womb. And he will turn many of the sons of Israel back to the Lord their God" (Luke 1:13b, 14b, 15b-16). Later, the Word reveals more concerning the same man, now a rustic, rugged messenger: "There came a man sent from God, whose name was John. He came as a witness, to testify about the light, so that all might believe through him" (John 1:6-7).

Further, to facilitate the spread of God's plan and message of redemption through Christ, God worked by calling some disciples: "And [Jesus] said to them, 'Follow Me, and I will make you fishers of men.' Immediately they left their nets and followed Him. Going on from there He saw two other brothers, . . . and He called them. Immediately they left the boat and their father, and followed Him" (Matthew 4:19-22). Later, Christ called the entire group of the twelve disciples: "And He went up on the mountain and summoned those whom He Himself wanted, and they came to Him. And He appointed twelve, so that they would be with Him, and that He could send them out to preach" (Mark 3:13-14).

In the ultimate formulation of the call narrative tradition in Scripture, much closer to contemporary ministers, God miraculously and marvelously called the apostle Paul, which he repeatedly referenced: "I thank Christ Jesus our Lord, who has strengthened me, because He considered me faithful, putting me into service" (1 Timothy 1:12).

Paul's identity and authority from God formed the basis of his spiritual leadership throughout his life, while punctuating the fullness of his ministry. He alluded to that divine call consistently in various epistles (see Romans 1:1; 1 Corinthians 1:1; 2 Corinthians 1:1; Galatians 1:1, etc.). In each case, the call from God validated God's specific leading in every supernatural undertaking.

We take further encouragement from Paul's words: "For if I preach the gospel, I have nothing to boast of, for I am under compulsion; for woe is me if I do not preach the gospel" (1 Corinthians

9:16). The call to preach involves an inner urge that one cannot resist. Ultimately, God has the final say in the matter of who will represent Him.

The cumulative importance of these call narratives is that they connect the contemporary called minister to those before, as well as others to follow, all in the will of the omnipotent God. When Christian ministers understand their calling and responsibility as indispensable to the divine plan, it underscores the supernatural dimension of the ministerial undertaking. Thus, one must never approach the divine calling from the perspective of biological legacy, moral merit, pride, flippancy, nor drudgery, nor sense of entitlement. If one approaches the call to preach in a cavalier, irreverent manner, the result will be a short, frustrating, and uneventful ministry.

On the other hand, if one embraces God's call to preach as a weighty, serious, grave matter and yields to that inner urge, the result will be complete satisfaction, peace, and fulfillment in life. Ultimately, the inability to resist the urge is a valuable litmus test for a divine call. Indeed, obedience to God always produces an indescribable peace with Him. That peace might often lie beyond human comprehension.

My own call experience in June 1978 was an extremely poignant moment. I had to filter through multiple impulses. 1) I had been reared in a Christian home. 2) In my local congregation, I appreciated the wisdom of Sunday school teachers, deacons, leaders, and dedicated parishioners. 3) I was a serious young man in that congregation. 4) I was very involved with Christian youth activities in my state. 5) I really wanted to "make something of myself" in the world as a college graduate, professional, and leader.

Therefore, because of these realities, many predicted that I would be a preacher. However, none of these considerations would do—for if I was destined by God to proclaim His Word, I would seek clear validation from Him.

Many internal stirrings and urges were coming forth. I can only sense them as the promptings of God. Whenever I spoke to youth groups, I had that sensation of doing the will of God. Yet, it was not fully formed within me.

Then a dear, godly saint heard me speak. She was adamant that I had been called by God. She called my mother to alert her of this fact. Initially, I could not be sure. Shortly thereafter, in sincere prayer, I asked God to make it real to me if it was, in fact, real. While in my college dormitory, I surrendered to an unusual disturbance within, a divine call, from which I have never turned away. When I surrendered to God's call to preach His Word, I made one request: "Father, please use me widely for Your glory."

Reflecting on the experience after more than thirty-seven years in Christian ministry, it was not cataclysmic, or mysterious, or spectacular. Instead, it was consistent with my relationship with God: when I sense He has spoken, I quietly and quickly obey Him. I usually do not spend inordinate time questioning God or myself. By nature, I am not loud, boisterous, or defiant. Nor am I normally reluctant, ambivalent, or overly inquisitive. Instead, I fervently seek God. Once I hear from Him in prayer, confirmed by the Word and by sincere saints of God, I have true peace.

The collective revelation from Scripture holds that one enters Christian ministry solely through specific assignment from God. This divine calling does not recognize the inherent standing, merit, goodness, ethics, or morality of the individual. Rather, it references the unequivocal will of God, most often beyond the imagination of the one called to lifelong Christian service. In simple terms: God calls to Christian ministry those whom He chooses for reasons that will only be fully revealed in eternity.

Once one receives confirmation from God in humble prayer, submitting to His will to preach the Word, the next step in the order of Christian movement must involve a candid conversation with one's pastor. (Yes, I assume that every called person is a devoted saint of God, growing in a Christian fellowship, under the spiritual covering of a called, anointed pastor.) The ultimate hope from this crucial conversation is to receive spiritual, biblical, and practical understanding of what God has called one to, and the steps to follow. That pastor then becomes one's spiritual father, uniquely situated to help this newly called Christian servant interpret the will of God for his/her life.

In the fall of 1978, I vividly recall my call conversation with my pastor. It was unremarkable, in that my pastor was very nonchalant as I explained my sense of God's call upon my life. In the privacy of his church office, my pastor heard me out without adding much to my biblical or professional understanding. I was even more confused as to what this meant.

I wondered if he considered me totally ill-suited or grossly unqualified for ministry. I further wondered if I had not uttered the right words to convey what I knew to be the new trajectory of my life. When I reported to my mother the contents of this conversation, she was full of questions: "What else did he say? When are you to preach your first message? What about seminary?" For each question, I was totally in the dark as to what came next.

Only later did my pastor reveal that in his experience, if one were truly called by God to Christian ministry, it was a decision and direction from which one could never turn away. Therefore, one should pray and pray again for certainty in this serious, engrossing, compelling, life-altering divine calling.

One Sunday night during worship, however, he made a statement that took me by total surprise: "Church, our boy, Jarvis Collier, has something to tell us. Come tell us, Son." In near shock, uncertain as to what to say, I went to the microphone. In the best way I could, I explained my sense of a call from God to preach His Word. That was it! Afterward, the congregation went into collective prayer for me. This unusual episode occurred after graduation from high school—the summer after my freshman year in college.

Before long, I would start my sophomore year at the University of California at Berkeley.

Because the summer months were so full, I never preached an initial sermon at my home church in Los Angeles. So I was somewhat adrift, unsure of my next step. Yet, once I was away at college, I joined another fellowship near the campus in Richmond, California.

There, after talking with my new pastor, I was scheduled to share this "trial" sermon in November of 1978. (That is the explanation for my having had two spiritual fathers.) Both shared excellent spiritual qualities: they were godly, Christ-exalting, Bible-centered, Holy Spirit-led, experienced, well-respected, dignified, staunch Baptist leaders, so much alike that they were wary of one another; yet, they both loved and nurtured me!

That initial sermon, drawn from 1 Corinthians 1:18-21, with the title, "Some Necessary Foolishness," was a most humbling experience. No one taught me how to prepare a biblical message. I did read some Bible commentaries, and I tried to emulate the preaching styles I had heard over so many years' time in the church. Some kind saints who heard the message said they were blessed. I am sure they were charitable in their evaluation of its merits. Still in Richmond, I submitted to worship, Sunday school, and growing in Christ among the saints there. After a few more opportunities to assess my sincerity in preaching and growing in biblical knowledge, I was given a license to preach the Gospel of Jesus Christ by my pastor and church family. This license meant that they shared a sense of my devotion to Christ, and a sense of a divine calling upon my life.

Later, I would transfer my studies, going home and enrolling at the University of California, Los Angeles (UCLA). Back home, I continued preaching for youth events at various churches. In a short time, I had several preaching engagements. Indeed, my popularity was spreading to the degree that I began to recommend friends to those invitations I could not fulfill. (In my immature preaching mind, I was on my way!) Again, I thank God for wise mentors, for there was still much to learn.

From two old-school, Baptist, conservative, wise, caring, godly fathers, I learned the value of sincerity in my walk with God. From the beginning, I saw in them serious commitment to Christ, leadership of the Holy Spirit, dedication to service, love for people, compassion for the community, and inexhaustible dedication to Christianity. They were resolute in prayer, worship, and spiritual distinction. For them, a Christian minister should always carry himself with faith, humility, dignity, integrity, and compassion for all humanity.

As one expression of Christian ministerial dignity, they wore dark suits, white shirts, and black shoes. In all things, they were the epitome of gravitas, decorum, dignity, and professionalism. (Perhaps due to personal style and age, today I wear dark suits, accented by blue, striped shirts, with white collars/white cuffs, and black shoes, maintaining dignity and decorum in dress as a minister of the Gospel of Jesus Christ.) In sartorial style, I reason in this manner: People should see in a Christian minister quiet humility, with dignity before God.

By and large, these fathers preached from the King James Version of the Bible. (Respectful of that tradition, I use the New American Standard Bible [NASB]. I believe it best captures historical, grammatical, theological, contextual, and pragmatic nuances of the Word, being especially beneficial for contemporary Christian and non-Christian audiences.)

They adhered to the central doctrines of the Christian faith: one God; authority of the Bible; one Savior; the virgin birth of Jesus; miracles of Christ; two church ordinances (baptism and the Lord's Supper); Christ's literal death, burial, and resurrection; literal heaven and hell; the imminent rapture of saints; and more.

So from the start, I was nurtured and grounded in the best of moral and theological development in Christ. Since then, nothing I have learned or been exposed to in seminaries, books, conferences, or conversations has shaken my foundation of faith in Christ alone, by grace alone, by faith alone to save all humanity willing to trust Christ.

In both subtle and overt ways, my fathers in Christ communicated their spiritual value system. Not surprisingly, that value system (biblical, Baptist, conservative) undergirded my perspective and worldview. I celebrate the priority of God's grace, prayer, worship, salvation through Christ alone, tithing, holiness, obedience, and sacrifice as central pillars of the Christian faith.

In matters large and small, then, I appreciate how God worked in my life, polishing my life through experiences with two tough, disciplined, and (as I said earlier) old-school fathers in the faith. That exposure was the crucible in which a spiritual life was shaped. It was the anvil on which a lifetime of truth was forged. Still, I hear their voices resoundingly in my inner ear. When I am tempted to do something that both would probably disagree with, I aim to defend it, reminded of some long-ago conversation we had. Today, then, if I cannot offer sufficient grounds for it, I usually abandon the idea because of such influence. Indeed, I ask myself, "What would Doc do in this situation?"

Additionally, my spiritual fathers were very kind and generous with their time and financial resources. I saw them provide for their families, their congregations, and those close to them. While in their presence, I never worried about my personal needs. Before I could ask, they were giving to me. At denominational gatherings, I deliberately spent time with one of them, knowing we would enjoy good restaurants together. (Yes, they paid the bill!) These godly men typified larger-than-life, opinionated, considerate, caring spirits. In fact, this spiritual trait was intimately connected with their conception of Christianity.

Later when both directed me toward graduate school (Christian seminary training), each contributed toward the financial support of my pursuits. In August 1981, I left Los Angeles with a Bachelor's degree, headed for Fort Worth, Texas, to attend Southwestern Baptist Theological Seminary, working toward a Master's degree there. Notice how David captured divine calling and personal preparation for godly service: "The steps of a man are established ("ordered" in the KJV) by the LORD, And He delights in his way" (Psalm 37:23).

In sharing their Christian perspective, each father emphasized the Word, the Spirit of God, and the supernatural, emphasizing the necessity of total reliance upon God for achieving anything of lasting significance. From their examples, I aspired to be a strong, dynamic, committed Christian minister and leader. They were true mentors, shaping the growing faith of an eager protégé.

As I reflect on my beginnings in Christian ministry, I am eternally grateful to God for giving me the particular fathers He did. In the spiritual realm, I feel akin to the Kennedys or the Rockefellers in the natural one. I am who I am because these godly men were gracious in granting me access, answering my "dumb" questions, exercising patience, fostering my lifelong yearning to grow in Christ, and giving glory to His holy name.

My pilgrimage of the Christian faith, as it relates to Christian ministry, reminds me of the protection these spiritual fathers gave to me. Their inputs resonate to this very hour.

In 2003, both of my spiritual fathers (Dr. E. V. Hill and Dr. A. H. Newman) were called home to rest eternally in the arms of the heavenly Father. It has taken me these intervening years to properly assess their exemplary, godly lifestyles in shaping me (and hundreds of others) in Christian character, devotion, leadership, and ministry for the kingdom of God through Christ.

The nostalgia of such remembrances fills me with immense joy and gratitude for these men of God serving as anointed obstetricians, birthing me in the maternity ward of Christian ministry. Later, they would continue to serve as deliberate pediatricians, as I attempted to walk in and talk the things of God.

So in a real sense, I have never felt abandonment, cynicism, or the need to make it on my own because these influences have always been present with and protective of me. Unwittingly, through God's grace, these spiritual mentors have prevented me from falling into ominous pitfalls along my journey, by offering books, wise counsel, direct intervention, encouragement, warning, pithy sayings, biting retort, or some other godly means of keeping me true to the calling of God.

Spiritual service to God and to humanity is never easy, but it is eased by spiritual patrons offering protective care in Jesus Christ. Due to their intentional interventions in my life, I have been preserved from my own inclinations. As true fathers, neither asked my permission to correct me when I veered from the proper path. At times, of course, I felt each was too strict on me, warning me of the pitfalls of ministry (hubris, lack of discipline, wavering prayer life, sexual impurity, alcohol, gambling, unwise use of money, and so forth). Yet, in hindsight, I wish they had stressed some lessons even more!

Additionally, I thank God that the human instruments used in my formation in Christ were tough, menacing, curmudgeon figures. Publicly, they were stoical; privately, they laughed while maintaining a distance. They communicated a vital lesson: "Be friendly, though not friends, with parishioners." As a pastor, I still abide by that subtle lesson.

Other spiritual lessons from those early days in ministry involved maintaining enthusiasm for proclaiming the eternal verities of Christ. I caught from them the need to always approach the opportunity to share the Word as if it were the first time, or the last time. God's people deserved, they explained, a preacher endowed with a timely and timeless message, grounded in Scripture, crystallized in Christ, anointed by God's Holy Spirit, directed toward a result.

Looking back, I am amazed at both the intellectual and spiritual depth of my two fathers in the faith. I truly marvel that they could consistently peek into the mysteries of God, bringing new, fresh insights from the written Word. In creative, anointed preaching, they brought the Word to life with commensurate applications for daily living. Each Sunday I (and hundreds of saints) heard the best of strong, anointed, creative, imaginative preaching. In my own way, it made me want to achieve the same through God's empowerment.

My two spiritual fathers were not formally seminary trained (for a variety of reasons). At the same time, they were voracious readers of the Bible, commentaries, newspapers, novels, and other sources of information. Despite the seeming disadvantage of the lack of seminary training, they relentlessly pushed me to give God my all, indicative of exemplary theological training. As far as they were concerned, I was going to seminary!

Once in seminary, I found it quite interesting the degree to which my godly fathers had conveyed lofty theological concepts, using only the Bible, prayer, anointing by God's Holy Spirit, self-directed readings, life experiences, wisdom, insight, common sense, and more. By whatever means, they were well ahead of their peers.

Mostly while in seminary I discovered new theoretical, esoteric, metaphysical, and polysyllabic means of saying what I had heard them declare from the earliest moments of Christian ministry. Indeed, they said and conveyed profound things about God in a simple fashion. (Yes, I am still learning how to emulate their example.) Often, I imagine their saying to me, "There must be a simple way to say that. So, say it that way!"

The major revelation from the divine call to a Christian minister involves conveying the lifelong nature of that calling. In a world of disposability after initial usage, many consider the call to Christian ministry as a temporary phase through which one passes. Not so with my spiritual fathers! They taught that nothing must interfere with the ministry. When you commit to Christian ministry, they said, you must remain true to God for the remainder of your life. If you cannot commit to such, do not start it. They put reverence for God in me, with the insistence, "There is dying in this business." (I interpreted that to mean dying to self-exertion, self-gratification, and self-aggrandizement.) Indeed, if one fails to preach, to serve, to go where God leads after being called, that person would die of utter frustration and futility.

Now, many may wish to dispute this notion, arguing that some can refuse to preach. In response, I have never met a fruitful, fulfilled, directed, successful person who willingly refused to obey God as a Christian minister. Once I met an ex-preacher whose face, words, and carriage depicted a sad, hollow, confused individual. Further, the Old Testament narrative of Jonah validates the impossibility of denying the will of God in ministry, while enjoying that willful disobedience. One may live a fruitless, meandering existence, but who would want that, and call it "living"?

Considering the totality of the call experience, early starts in Christian ministry, and all that pertains to a new venture in the kingdom of God, we should profusely thank God for protective, compassionate, patient spiritual fathers. Elders in the faith recognize vulnerabilities, insecurities, naiveté, incessant questions, and more as young clergy grapple with the enormity of the Christian leadership task ahead of them.

No wonder that God counseled Joshua, not long after charging him with leadership of the recently emancipated Jewish slaves: "Be strong and courageous, for you shall give this people possession of the land which I swore to their fathers to give them. Only be strong and very courageous; be careful to do according to all the law which Moses My servant commanded you; do not turn from it to the right or to the left, so that you may have success wherever you go" (Joshua 1:6-7). Notably, "strength" and "courage" would be key components for a leadership paradigm of successfully taking God's people forward.

Indeed, if not for the protection of godly fathers reminding sons and daughters in the faith of the sovereignty of God amid every conceivable challenge, many young clergy would become untimely casualties, with their wasted potential on full display.

In the end, unfortunately, protective spiritual fathers cannot protect their progeny from all tests, trials, and tragedies. Indeed, younger clergy often ruin potentially meaningful ministries through sinful indulgences (enumerated earlier). True mentors in Christ will, however, render aid in any scenario, reminding sons and daughters in Christian ministry that the best from God and for God lies just over the next horizon. More than cliché, some of us live with the notion that the best remains yet to come! So we toil on toward the triumph of our faith, knowing that failure is never final; defeat is not definitive; perplexity is passing; adversity is for a while; and God will always bring us through!

Yet, for the most part, God has engineered the circumstances of a healthy, protective mentor-protégé relationship in such a way that spiritual covering by a father in the faith will decrease the likelihood of ministerial failure. Such a providentially arranged, divinely orchestrated relationship greatly advances the kingdom of God through the Lord, Jesus Christ.

9

THE PROVISION OF A SPIRITUAL FATHER

It has been the driving thesis of this book that a spiritual father, a godly mentor, occupies singular significance in shaping younger Christian leaders and the congregations they serve. Research into this thesis has been immeasurably augmented by dialogue with, and analysis of, the career trajectory of fifteen Christian father figures. Each man has achieved at least fifty years in Christian ministry, with notable national successes. They completed written responses to a survey, asking their views on a variety of topics.

By provision here, I wish to appreciate the work of God in developing spiritual fathers of character, integrity, wisdom, compassion, courage, grace, and insight. By instilling such values, traits, and principles in men profiled throughout this book, God has produced the present generation with worthy models of Christian excellence. So faith leaders today are without excuse, as we aim to fulfill a tremendous responsibility in representing God as His instruments, giving deference to Christ in the expansion of God's kingdom.

In so many ways, spiritual mentors validate the assertion that there is no real success without a successor. Thus, after an eventful ministry, each can rest well in the knowledge of their spiritual legacy continuing in spiritual sons and daughters. Legacies are formed and fostered while men are working for Christ, often unaware of the lengthening shadow of their influence.

When a young cleric has delivered the Word of God with coherence, anointing, fervor, and scholarship while extolling Christ as Savior, among African-American Christian leaders I have heard it said, "Friends, after hearing a message like that, the Lord's church rests in good hands." I exegete that comment to mean that each generation must take the Christ message, develop it for present times, and then pass it on to bless future generations.

Against that backdrop I sought out wise spiritual fathers, godly mentors, because I wanted to gauge their responses to many of the seminal issues roiling Christian circles across the denominational spectrum: the nature of salvation; worship practices; music; marriage challenges; the role of congregations in social justice; abortion; absentee fathers; the megachurch phenomenon; technology; political engagement; and more. Kindly, they sent back their responses.

They were unanimous in affirming biblical orthodoxy amid cataclysmic shifts in our culture. If sincere saints of God desire greater kingdom impact in our culture, we must embrace biblical principles rather than compromising with all individuals, ideologies, and institutions. As sanctified "salt" (see Matthew 5:13), Christians preserve their society. Spiritual fathers are critical in constantly reminding this generation of its responsibility before God.

Rather than seeking to accommodate the human tendency to reshape God to our limited dimensions, these fathers held that, on the contrary, life must be lived according to His stipulations. Indeed for them, saints of God must accept His prescriptions for life if the relationship is to benefit us. Throughout this book, I have littered chapters with their insights.

Something fundamental, in my view, is forever lost as current Christian leaders forsake wisdom from God, faith, sober analysis, biblical insight, prayerfulness, faithfulness, experience, length of Christian service, gray hair, wrinkles, shortened steps, reflection on past victories, and more from spiritual fathers. These men have accrued invaluable treasure from walking with God, like Enoch in Genesis 5:21-24, that must be passed on to the next generation. Spiritual fathers, then, are expected to pass the torch of faith, while sons and daughters are expected to receive it, all for the advancement of the kingdom of God through our Savior, Jesus Christ.

Moreover, I was intrigued by the biblical exhortation from the minor prophet in the Old Testament: "Your old men will dream dreams, Your young men will see visions" (Joel 2:28b). Within all that shall take place associated with the second advent of Christ (still to come in history), Joel prophesied that older men would revisit moments of ecstasy, filled with epiphanies from God (dreams), while younger leaders would see infinite potential (visions) in accord with fidelity to God. Perhaps this explains the oft-seen Christian leadership dichotomy: older clergy "dream" backwards, while younger ones "vision" forward. Both, however, are necessary for the advancement of the kingdom of God through Christ.

The best measure of a person's life will never be quantified by material resources; but it can be celebrated in those he/she helped to realize their full potential. In short, mature people give themselves to enduring causes and important challenges, becoming champions of meaningful endeavors. Well-remembered leaders are those who pursue worthy initiatives, often caring little for personal acclaim. Instead, they leave an enduring legacy in the legions who recall their life calling.

For example, the American Civil Rights Movement led by Dr. Martin Luther King Jr. represented a watershed moment in achieving a higher degree of equality, freedom, and justice for African Americans in particular and all of America in general. Dr. King as a personal mentor can be seen in protégés who went on to national/global renown (Jesse Jackson, Andrew Young, John Lewis, and many others).

Moreover, mentors foreshadow success in protégés in varied disciplines and important fields of endeavor. As an example, in the 2014 college basketball tournament dubbed "March Madness," it was noted in several publications that Rick Pitino, famed basketball coach at the University of Louisville, served as the mentor to many younger coaches in the same tournament. The articles pointed out the strange sensation of a protégé coaching against a mentor, with each sorely aiming to win a national championship.

Yet, the deeper revelation I took from the unique situation was that in most cases, the younger coach could never have served as a reputable coach if not for the tutelage, influence, and body of knowledge gained from serving under a father figure, such as coaching legend Pitino. Throughout forty-plus years at various levels, Pitino has been successful, designing offensive and defensive schemes, honing players' skills, and teaching basketball fundamentals. In turn, his coaching ways have been copied, modified, and adapted by his protégés around America. Indeed, university presidents, athletic directors, and others, knowing one's connection to and now pedigree of Pitino, feel quite comfortable when hiring that new coach.

Such thinking involves the "reflected glory" scenario: surely, some intangibles from the mentor will inevitably rub off on the protégé. In the Old Testament, the great emancipator Moses was mandated to put some of his authority on God's designated successor, Joshua (see Numbers 28:18-20). From that moment onward, Joshua was being meticulously groomed by Moses to serve God and His people with integrity, courage, dignity, patience, prayerfulness, and adherence to and total absorption in the divine plan. That leadership paradigm of mentor-protégé should still serve in the perpetuation of God's agenda for redeemed humanity.

In my own walk with God, I have found Joshua to be a riveting, compelling, intriguing character in Scripture. I have studied his life and ministry before God, keenly aware that many of us today in Christian ministry will function in the shadow of those who accomplished meaningful exploits for God. I have gleaned deeper insight about the body of Christ from Joshua's godly leadership. As protégés faithfully stand on mentors' shoulders, God allows our spiritual perspective to be enhanced.

Further in the New Testament, we observe that the Son of God came to earth for the specific purpose of reconciling humanity to the heavenly Father. Importantly, Christ was aided in His earthly ministry by twelve disciples. These footstep followers of Christ literally and figuratively basked in His glory.

Throughout three years of intense exposure to the Lord of life, they worked side-by-side with the One sent by God to redeem sinful humanity. The disciples' curriculum entailed watchfulness, listening to His declarations, analyzing their ideals, participating in miracles, and then sharing sublime revelation from the heavenly Father mediated through His Son. Their training by Christ was all for the benefit of alienated humanity. And, we should recall, it all began with the critical relationship of mentor (Christ) and His maturing protégés (twelve disciples).

Further, corporate America furnishes other examples of wise mentors helping to mold future generations of successful leaders in finance, banking, commodities trading, leveraged buyouts, IPOs, and the spectrum of products offered by businesses. Most young leaders tie their rapid rise through the ranks of corporate America to the experience, exposure, and time/energy investment of a father figure. Through invaluable exchanges of knowledge and inquiry, such careers are forged.

Accordingly, spiritual mentors provide through varied means.

1. EXTOLLING THE CENTRAL TENETS OF CHRISTIANITY

Those in Christian leadership need constant reminders of their divine calling, their duties before God, and their indisputable influence for good as they set the agenda for today's Christian witness. When leaders are without a vision from God (strengthened by exposure to strong, godly, accomplished spiritual fathers), they revert to outmoded functions, traditional analysis, maintenance ministry, or mimicry of celebrated models, never developing their full identity as Christian leaders.

In many cases, to our shame, it is possible to sit through a Christian worship service without hearing a clear presentation of the Christian Gospel. In its place, we are too often entertained rather than being empowered; made to feel good, rather than being reminded of God's grace (in Christ); and told of positive benefits of life (marriage, career, prosperity, promotion, ease, and more).

For me, based on the spiritual fathers who shaped my development, I stand on the importance of clearly articulating the name and nature of our Savior. Increasingly, my Christ-centered dogmatism is founded in Scripture: "For I determined to know nothing among you except Jesus Christ, and Him crucified" (1 Corinthians 2:2). That Christ perspective—narrow for some, deemed bigoted by others, yet beneficial for all—should characterize the widely embraced proclamation from pulpits across America and the world.

2. REMINDERS OF THE "MAIN THING"

Spiritual fathers, further, reiterate the importance of remaining true to biblical, spiritual, and relational principles: worship, prayer, faith, obedience, love, moral deportment, integrity, transparency, and faithfulness to God. Nothing in the Word of God commends silliness, frivolity, or frolicking through life by leaders; so spiritual fathers must continually point up the gravity of the work of the kingdom of God.

While many Christian ministers do quite well in the preaching dimension of their work, an equal number fail in establishing the central mission of Christ (making disciples). In the process, many congregations meet with regularity without due consideration of the daily and eternal plight of the unsaved world just outside their hallowed sanctuary. It is the job, I contend, of Christian leaders to chart a course centered in Christian evangelism.

Clearly, numerous Christian congregations are losing membership support, resulting in meager resources. Others are dealing with members advancing in age, while others are passing away. Millions see the same trend lines, without a means of rectifying a bad situation. Others, viewing negative trends for Christianity, recognize the constant need for renewed emphases. Somehow, we must call millions to evangelism and discipleship. Somewhere I heard it well stated, "The Christian church is always just one generation away from extinction."

Venues for reaching unsaved people for Christ are manifold: post offices, banks, malls, airport lounges, coffee shops, movie theaters, supermarkets, jobsites, service stations, shoeshine stands, barbershops, hair salons, and everywhere people gather.

3. GOAD TO GIVING GOD ONE'S BEST

Spiritual fathers, moreover, are consequential in fostering an environment intolerant of offering God the average, the mediocre, the "whatever." Instead, younger clergy must always feel goads to offer God and His church one's best. So pivotal mentors in the faith will champion sanctification, holiness, discipline, and godliness. In so doing, they ensure that the next generation savors the privilege of representing God before humanity. Famously, Paul instructed the saints in godliness: "Therefore I urge you, brethren, by the mercies of God, to present your bodies a living and holy sacrifice, acceptable to God, which is your spiritual service of worship" (Romans 12:1). Also, he made the matter plain: "be holy both in body and spirit" (1 Corinthians 7:34).

In evangelical Christianity, none should negotiate away fundamental principles—orthodoxy—in hopes of wide cultural acceptance. In short, saints of God must often take and continually maintain a principled, biblical stance for all that aligns with divine truth. Led by strong Christian fathers, the Christian minister must never waver from the core values of the Christian witness. Famously, a mature Christ-follower, Peter, advised saints, "[B]ut sanctify Christ as Lord in your hearts, always being ready to make a defense to everyone who asks you to give an account for the hope that is in you, yet with gentleness and reverence" (1 Peter 3:15).

In that instance, as the denier of the Savior then turned Pentecost-preacher, Peter stood as a Christian apologist, exhorting the Christian faithful to defend the faith, lest it suffer from critics, skeptics, scoffers, and others. Because he was quite familiar with losing heart in the midst of severe challenge, Peter advised all against such weak posture.

In practical terms, fathers in the faith should relish their roles in reminding younger Christian leaders that they represent the gracious, loving God of the universe. That divine love for humanity was on sterling display in His sending His Son as the Savior. Those graciously called by God to convey that Christ message should, accordingly, represent the kingdom of God, operating from the highest standards of devotion, character, and love for Him.

4.   STAY "THERE" THROUGHOUT ANOTHER'S JOURNEY

In the natural realm, true fathers remain a physical, emotional, financial, and relational presence in the lives of their children. (Some fathers reading this might say some children remain financially dependent too long!) What I advocate is similar but far more significant: by the grace of God, spiritual fathers should remain present in the lives of their progeny in Christ, at least until the younger minister reaches spiritual maturity. In my experience, it seems that God removed "Elijah" as "Elisha" became fully prepared to minister in his own right (see 2 Kings 2:1-12). Graciously, God ensured that the coveted "mantle" was left behind for Elisha's benefit.

Today, spiritual fathers play a significant role, being "there" during times of personal stress, brokenness, and failure for younger clergy. Such fathers demonstrate and wonderfully express the grace, mercy, and love of God for those ensnared in ill-advised choices, dilemmas, and questionable alliances. Such fathers create an environment for beneficial dialogue, as inner resources prove futile and doubts multiply.

Further, godly fathers provide counsel to wounded counselors. Where do godly helpers turn when they, in fact, need help? The answer is clear: godly mentors refocus Christian ministry for those devastated by debt, divorce, doubt, or a fatal decision. Sensing younger clergy as invaluable for advancing the kingdom of God, godly mentors help reassemble the fragments of ministry after all seems lost. In fact, I believe God places them in one's life precisely for that purpose.

5. MAINTAIN FOCUS AMID ALLURES

Endowed with a heightened, seasoned, godly perspective, spiritual mentors assist younger clergy in maintaining focus amid an array of allures: success and status, fame and fortune, charisma and celebrity. In the twenty-first century, so many younger Christian leaders take cues from a confused culture, forgetting their calling from God and the need to honor Him by remaining clear on the work to which they have been called: extolling the name of Christ, thereby extending the privilege of sharing in the kingdom of God.

As a native of Los Angeles and as a Christian preacher, in some ways I am ashamed of the guilt by association inherent in the televised reality series *Preachers of Los Angeles*. While I know several of the participants, applaud their successes, and respect their commitment to God, I fear that, unwittingly, they leave viewers with a sense of trivial concerns by Christian ministers (opulent residences, flashy vehicles, jewelry, fame, prosperity, pettiness, and so forth), when our true calling involves invading spiritual darkness with the light of Jesus Christ.

Without going on a tirade, my concern is that too many people will use this series and any other reason to forsake the community of faith: "See, many ministers are only in ministry for the money, so I don't go to any church" is a refrain I have heard on countless occasions.

So fathers in the faith must tether younger clerics to awesome responsibility before God above all other enticements. Ministers serve as the watchmen for the souls of the saved (see Ezekiel 3:17; Hebrews 13:17). Truly, someone must serve as the fatherly corrective for the excesses of twenty-first-century Christian ministry (private jets, naked financial appeals, "prosperity gospel," and blatant hucksterism).

6.   GODLY MENTORS SERVE AS SOUNDING BOARDS

In shaping ministers under their spiritual care, godly fathers exemplify lifelong mentoring by serving as sounding boards for younger leaders. Often, the latter possess a flood of ideas, aiming to make a considerable impact using the latest trends, in a technocentric world given over to the pragmatic, at the expense of well-founded biblical principles. Sometimes younger clergy, enamored of the trendy, fail to embrace established theological conclusions.

Against these notions, fathers in the faith offer tests before taking action: prayerfulness, deep reflection, breadth of analysis, faithfulness to God, and maintaining Christ as the center of all truth while weighing propositions for their long-term implications. Not surprisingly, such fathers assert the wisdom inherent in statements like "haste makes waste," or, "Rome was not built in a day." These clichés rebut popular ideas associated with speed, effect, and initial valuation. Simply put, success in Christian ministry and concomitant important Christian endeavors occur over time.

How many Christian congregations could have been spared terrible decisions if only their young leaders had shared their dreams with older spiritual mentors prior to offering them to congregants? At this point, it might be helpful to add that seminaries prepare graduates to lead congregations, while mentors help shape the parameters of what is feasible for those churches. An older colleague puts it in this way: "I may not know a winning strategy for every church disturbance, but I can help someone avoid getting into a fracas in the first place." Part of that answer is that leaders must stand for non-negotiable principles while leaving trivial matters alone, as such will ultimately work themselves out.

7. SUSTENANCE FOR CHRISTENDOM

Finally, godly mentors provide sustenance for Christendom because God invests in individuals, transforming them in Christ, making them part of His church. The best of God's investment in His creation is best exemplified in His sending His only begotten Son as Savior of all who trust Him in faith. In addition, the objective of sending Christ was to advance God's kingdom.

Incredibly, God stakes much on feeble, flawed, finite creatures. Further, in every generation since Christ's advent—more than two millennia and counting—God has called, anointed, and sent men and women to convey His abiding love and rescuing grace to estranged, sinful, fractured humanity. Paul's rhetorical embellishment of that truth captures us: "How then will they call on Him in whom they have not believed? How will they believe in Him whom they have not heard? And how will they hear without a preacher? How will they preach unless they are sent?" (Romans 10:14-15a).

As spiritual fathers reach an age and stage of Christian maturity and godly influence, they are positioned to impact future generations for God's glory. The apostle Paul, the embodiment of a spiritual father, captured the essence of this responsibility from God: "The things which you have heard from me in the presence of many witnesses, entrust these to faithful men who will be able to teach others also" (2 Timothy 2:2).

10

THE PROMOTION OF A SPIRITUAL FATHER

Christian life, ministry, and generations of leaders all tremendously benefit from spiritual mentors who willingly promote the interests of protégés as protégés demonstrate potential, character, integrity, ability, dedication, and intellect within a godly life trajectory. In fact, this spiritual transfer represents part of the divine design to ensure a legacy of fidelity: "So the LORD said to Moses, 'Take Joshua the son of Nun, a man in whom is the Spirit, and lay your hand on him; and have him stand before Eleazar the priest and before all the congregation, and commission him in their sight. You shall put some of your authority on him, in order that all the congregation of the sons of Israel may obey him'" (Numbers 27:18-20). In the vernacular of today, Moses was given the assignment of the equivalent of writing a letter of recommendation to the "pastoral search committee" of Israel. In effect, Moses the Lawgiver was offering a sterling character reference of his longtime protégé, Joshua.

To polish this promotional notion, I wish to conduct a thought experiment. In the evaluation of current Christian leaders (pastors, theologians, denominational executives, authors, commentators, lecturers, and more), we might ask some important questions: "Who was his/her mentor before he/she became prominent?" "Who saw a smidgen of potential in her, and honed it toward something special?" "Who knew, early on, that he could lead others?" "Who might have provided a small platform, allowing him to be heard before ever-widening audiences?"

As I pose these questions, I trust that by now it exposes the very premise of this book: spiritual fathers matter! They represent wise, dignified, faithful, and godly patrons seeing in persons much more than they might see in themselves for the greater glory of God. As patrons, they expend a great deal of time, energy, and revenue pushing another toward his or her best. By design, these fathers foster opportunities for their progeny to shine in the brilliance of the right introduction, at the right time, in the right moment.

Once I heard a godly father speak of a son in Christ in this way: "He represents a quality piece of cloth marked out for big things; we must help to 'sew him up.'"

Indeed, I seek answers to the following:

- Who saw something unique in Billy Sunday, Billy Graham, D. Elton Trueblood, Vance Havner, and Charles Fuller well before each came into his own?

- Who nurtured Christian proclivities inherent in Charles Stanley, Chuck Swindoll, Chuck Colson, Bill Bright, D. James Kennedy, and Jerry Falwell, foreseeing infinite possibilities before they became apparent to all?

- Who celebrated unusual promise in Martin Luther King Jr., Gardner C. Taylor, Joseph H. Jackson, C. A. W. Clark, D. E. King, Leon Sullivan, William Jones, Frederick Sampson, Samuel Proctor, and E. V. Hill prior to their launch on the national and global stage?

- Who pushed, prodded, and promoted the life and works of esteemed voices in Christendom, such as Donald Hilliard, Paul Morton, W. Franklyn Richardson, Ralph West, Freddy Haynes, Frank Reid III, Neil Ellis, Kenneth Ulmer,

Maurice Watson, Lance Watson, Clarence McClendon, James Meeks, Joseph Walker, Freddy Clark, Jerry Young, Jamal Bryant, H. B. Charles Jr., Walter Thomas, Darrell Hines, Jack Vaughn, and Calvin Butts both before and since their ascent?

- Who noticed the unproven yet unassailable giftings of Kenneth Hagin Sr., Oral Roberts, Benny Hinn, Lester Sumrall, and R. W. Shambach before television, radio, Internet, and world conference fame?

- Who championed the ministries of Tony Evans, T. D. Jakes, Joel Osteen, Eddie Long, Creflo Dollar, I. V. Hilliard, Charles Blake, Max Lucado, and Rick Warren while each toiled in anonymity before reaching national acclaim?

In the aforementioned cited examples, the point is that someone, somewhere—a kind patron, a spiritual mentor, a father in the faith—went out of his way to actively promote (like a selfless cheerleader) the life and ministry of one who, by the grace of God, would occupy a wider bearing in Christendom if given the proper circumstances. Often, this element of spiritual influence is forgotten by the recipient, as so many claim that their place of prominence came as the result of their own rigorous exertion.

While we may not know the names of the patrons, the godly mentors, and the spiritual fathers, we do know that their investment in unknown persons has handsomely paid rich dividends for the kingdom of God through Christ, to the glory of God. In economic terms, their ROI (return-on-investment) has been phenomenal!

It has been the driving thesis of this book that spiritual fathers—godly mentors—occupy singular significance in helping shape younger Christian leaders and the congregations they serve.

In another field—broadcast journalism—the same truth applies. In the halcyon days of television, Walter Cronkite was the gold standard of news anchors. So-called the "most trusted man in America," Cronkite set a high bar to which young journalists strained to reach. One of Cronkite's acolytes, Bob Schieffer, at 77, still idolizes him as a mentor, guide, and friend. As for Schieffer, his best days seem to have been those after age 65; he has moderated three presidential debates, written three books, anchored CBS nightly news, and hosted its *Face the Nation* program, along with surviving bladder cancer!

Perhaps we should make a judgment call: successful people have mentors!

Further, in the New Testament we observe that the Son of God came to earth for the specific purpose of reconciling humanity to the heavenly Father. Importantly, Christ was aided in His earthly ministry by twelve disciples. These footstep followers of Christ literally and figuratively basked in His glory. Throughout three years of intense exposure to the Lord of life, they were allowed to work side-by-side with the One sent by God to redeem sinful humanity.

The twelve disciples' training by Christ was to benefit alienated humanity. Even as they were still naïve regarding His ultimate mission, right before His ascension (see Acts 1:6), they needed rigorous teaching from the Savior. And, we should recall, it all began with the critical relationship of mentor (Christ) and maturing protégés (twelve disciples).

In analyzing Christ's relationships with the Twelve, both collectively and individually, it must have been maddening and exasperating to note what was taught them over against the measure of their understanding, even after three years of intense training. Yet, that is the model for spiritual fathers relating to younger clergy. Often, fathers may be driven to wonder, "Why is it so difficult for him/her to understand this?" But through tenacity to the responsibility of mentorship, spiritual mentors promote others by multiple means.

1. CHALLENGING PRESUPPOSITIONS

I recall a spiritual father who, on several occasions, challenged my thinking. He would ask me to evaluate something in the current news, a message we had just heard, or some proposition. His method of challenging me was a Socratic one—a series of disquieting questions. If I answered with affirmation or enthusiasm, he would meticulously show me its deficiencies. Then I would understand that what appears to be solid, sturdy, and strong may in fact be constructed on a slippery foundation.

In that episode, and countless others, he was shaping and reshaping my cultural filters, enlarging my prism so that I could see there were several ways to interpret what I assumed was reality. In the end, he wanted me to employ the Word of God, with Jesus Christ its apex, the supernatural, and advancement of God's kingdom its highest priority. Those considerations, he made clear, should serve as my ultimate standard of judgment.

2. PROMOTING IMAGINATION WITHIN THE BOUNDS OF SCRIPTURE

All Christian clergy must ask themselves, "With whom do I converse?" "What forms the basis of my conversations?" "After they are over, what am I inspired to achieve?" "Is God glorified by my daily works?" Some of these matters are honed and burnished through intentional interactions with godly father figures.

The prototype of a spiritual father is one who is accessible to younger clergy as a loving, dedicated, helpful, nonjudgmental asset in their times of crisis, conflict, and challenge. For all spiritual fathers aspiring to that level of acclaim and affirmation, it is useful to practice the job before obtaining the title!

So many younger clergies exist on conversations with peers, longing for a time of influence, while spiritual fathers rely upon decades in service to God and His people. These are two very different perspectives. While the younger speculates on what could be, the older reflects on what has already been achieved for the advancement of the kingdom of God.

3. REMIND ALL TO PAY IT FORWARD

The late Dr. E. K. Bailey of Dallas (a young spiritual father who, in my view, passed away too soon), helped a younger minister through a financial challenge as the minister sought to enroll in seminary. With gratitude, the minister promised to repay Dr. Bailey. Instead, Pastor Bailey replied, at some point, that when it goes well to simply assist another young person in a similar moment. That is the wisdom of a spiritual father.

The principle of reciprocity goes a long way in explaining why some succeed while others fail. Also, by sowing a seed, saints of God ensure a harvest from God. That represents the bedrock, irrevocable truth: "While the earth remains, seedtime and harvest, And cold and heat, And summer and winter, And day and night Shall not cease" (Genesis 8:22).

At some point, in my view, a dangerous mindset develops within some clergy, even spiritual fathers. In seeking to toughen others for the rigors of Christian life, leadership, and ministry, a father figure might conclude, "Well, nobody helped me, and I made it. So, you must achieve the best way you can!"

That philosophy—cold, mean-spirited, secular, selfish, wrong, repugnant, vile, ignorant, and ungodly—should be rejected! In fact, every person on this planet has been helped by a multitude of others, starting from birth and continuing until death. Therefore, each of us is obligated to pay it forward.

Around the year 1986, while leading a small congregation in Los Angeles, a well-known pastor there, a spiritual mentor, brought his choir, ushers, leaders, and members to share with us, supporting our meager group during an afternoon worship. Afterward, I asked him what financial remuneration I might give him. He declined anything!

Later, I had the chance to pay it forward, duplicating his act in encouraging the life of a pastor and small congregation in Kansas City. My honorarium that night was zero! I praise God for the opportunity of giving back as it had been done for me. And the cycle should continue, ad infinitum.

4. EXPRESS GOD'S USE OF ORDINARY PEOPLE FOR HIS GLORY

Equally vital, godly mentors are critical because God invests so much in His church, providing her with quality leaders, both young and old.

So the cumulative takeaway from exploring the promotional role of a spiritual father should reveal that spiritual fathers can help advance one's ministerial career far better than he or she can alone. Godly mentors operate from a position of objectivity, able to offer critique based on verifiable criteria. In most cases, they would rather tell the truth than gloss over areas in need of considerable work.

It takes very little to offer a career boost to another. Corporate titans do it; political leaders do it; entertainers do it; standup comics do it, coaches do it. So here is the big question: "Are there enough Christian leaders in the land willing to open a door for others?"

5. EVALUATE INDIVIDUALS' HEARTS, RATHER THAN SCHOLARSHIP ALONE

The true barometer of an individual, especially a Christian minister, cannot be discerned from surface appraisals. Tall, muscular, witty, charismatic, sharp, loquacious, and helpful represent superficial traits. In a deeper way, we need to see evidence of one's new birth experience, fruit of the Spirit, integrity, discipline, devotion, prayerfulness, biblical depth, scholarship, anointing, resoluteness, and sincerity of purpose.

Also, early indicators of promise often cannot foretell multiple potential pitfalls of Christian ministry. In a word, those who flash across the sky like meteors may not possess the spiritual discipline required for the long haul. Again, ministry is never a sprint; rather, it resembles a marathon. Only those who can endure will enjoy its sweet nectar.

Spiritual fathers, then, must ask God for clarity in determining whom they should promote. We should recall this Scripture verse: "Do not look at his appearance or at the height of his stature, because I have rejected him; for God sees not as man sees, for man looks at the outward appearance, but the LORD looks at the heart" (1 Samuel 16:7).

6. MOTIVATE OTHERS TOWARD PROFESSIONAL
   ATTAINMENT

Within the surveys I conducted of spiritual fathers, I discovered that most spent considerable time daily at their churches or seminary offices. Because they viewed Christian ministry as a special calling from God, they felt it important to be available to their parishioners or students. None can ever know the full range of challenges and emergencies people might face. Consequently, like an attorney or medical doctor, the office lends itself to notable achievement.

I recognize that with technology all feel at all times connected, whether at their home offices, a restaurant, on the golf course, at the gym, or wherever. Yet, many saints of God feel they are part of something spiritually significant because the leader deems it important to maintain regular office hours.

Permit me to state the matter bluntly: lazy, unfocused, confused leaders will produce the same in their followers. Conversely, leaders holding to high standards will produce the same in their followers. I tell my small church staff, "You represent God, His kingdom, this fellowship, me, and yourselves. Please make efficiency and excellence the hallmark of every effort."

Within this setting, of course, members and students should adhere to professional policies: 1) exemplify Christ in all matters; 2) pray before you proceed; 3) call for an appointment; 4) keep the appointment; 5) succinctly state your business; 6) remain optimistic regarding the outcome; 7) leave a message or a return phone number with the secretary/receptionist; 8) appreciate the load leaders operate under; 9) cooperate with others; 10) trust God, no matter what!

On the other hand, Christian leaders should daily dress and comport themselves as consummate professionals. During the week, this means wearing if not a suit, then at least a dress shirt or nice sweater, slacks, and dress shoes for a man; a demure dress/skirt/top and low heels for a woman. Perhaps the absence of spiritual fathers has allowed too much casual attire to be worn by young Christian leaders.

The key concept I assert is the confidence fostered by leaders through their decency, decorum, and dignity. Note Paul's exhortation to Timothy as a subtle push toward professional representation in Christian ministry: "And he (overseer, bishop, pastor) must have a good reputation with those outside the church, so that he will not fall into reproach and the snare of the devil" (1 Timothy 3:7).

A few simple suggestions for professional offices (especially Christian ones) will enhance work for God's kingdom advance: 1) Regular pastor/professor office hours; 2) Human voice answering the phone; 3) Staff office hours; 4) Standard for all—requests made in written form; 5) Widely published church office phone and fax numbers and e-mail addresses; 6) Regular written reports—membership, students, constituency; 7) Decent, dignified dress in the office; 8) Emphasis on godliness, courtesy, and excellence; 9) Clean, neat work areas; 10) Timely return of all calls.

7. ENCOURAGE THOSE WITH CHARACTER AND INTEGRITY TO THE FULLEST

In various ecclesiological traditions, particularly Baptists with congregational polity, ministers submit an application for leadership of a congregation. Somewhere in that application, the pastoral search committee may ask for letters of recommendation, most often from respected Christian figures. Typically, one letter might come from an esteemed, godly father figure. Depending on his influence (local, national, global), it may immeasurably sway the candidate's prospects, prompting the committee to forward a favorable recommendation of his/her name to the entire church body.

Indeed, I give congregations this warning: If you are seriously considering a candidate for the pastorate of your congregation, that minister should first have a strong, vibrant relationship with God. Then, the candidate should have similar devotion to his pastor. That father figure should provide a thorough evaluation to your committee of that candidate's conversion experience, maturity in Christ, biblical perspective, marital status, credit history, personal maturity, integrity, dependability, work ethic, record in the church, schools attended, degrees received, and honors bestowed.

Indeed, that spiritual mentor should literally be willing to stake his well-earned reputation on the viability of that candidate. If this pastor/leader/denominational figure will not unreservedly give that candidate his highest ranking, your congregation should view it as a red flag, perhaps in itself disqualifying the prospective pastor.

Decades ago, my beloved pastor Dr. E. V. Hill, in a similar situation, told me to write my own recommendation letter. I did so—and he read it, asked his secretary to put it on his church stationery, and then sent it away. By God's grace, I was called to serve as pastor/senior minister of that particular church!

11

THE PERSPECTIVE OF A SPIRITUAL FATHER

As the years elapse, it seems as though one after another, with regular frequency, prominent spiritual fathers are called home to the heavenly Father. In April 2015, the Christian world received news of the spiritual transition of the "Dean of American Preachers," Dr. Gardener C. Taylor. In his passing, Christians lamented the felling of a giant oak tree in God's forest. King David, weeping over Saul and Jonathan, said it well: "Tell it not in Gath, proclaim it not in the streets of Ashkelon," . . . "How have the mighty fallen in the midst of the battle!" (2 Samuel 1.20a, 25a). His legacy, however, will bless Christendom for generations to come.

In a spiritual father's absence, we reflect upon their singular achievements. As the grace of God allows, I have attended several memorials as a way of acknowledging their dedication to Christ, legacy of leadership, contributions to the kingdom, and influence in my life. With sadness over their passing, we remark to Christian colleagues the broad trajectory of their influence in God's kingdom advancement. Hearing encomiums heaped upon them after a lifetime of dedicated service to God and humanity, intelligent younger clerics should aspire toward a similarly substantive journey of faith.

Yet, this book asks that we properly assess what made such men true spiritual fathers, rather than simply older ministers. In every professional discipline (journalism, the arts, academia, science, medicine, literature, corporate, and so on), there are luminaries who exhibit great gifts. After they pass on, few of us analyze their legacy for clues on enhancing our own effectiveness.

I am particularly at a loss in such transitions because my generation (Christian ministers ages 50–65) celebrated a unique connection with such godly fathers. Faithfully, we walked with the fathers, heard their messages, adhered to their insights, and digested their leadership paradigms. Looking back fondly, some of us apprenticed under great spiritual leaders: as briefcase holders, gofers, and those who performed other insignificant tasks. (Before the concept of an armor-bearer became potent in African-American Christian circles, some of us simply served!). In the process, God sharpened us for future ministerial leadership. Indeed, as good followers, I pray that many of us have been, and are being, made into useful servants for the kingdom of our Lord.

What are the best traits forming spiritual fathers' perspective?

1. MEN OF SPIRITUAL SUBSTANCE

Those who shaped my pastoral thought, philosophy of ministry, vision for engagement, and dreams for the body of Christ could easily be characterized as larger than life. Several were bold, controversial, opinionated, brash, and strong in their views. I respected them in the moment for taking tough stands, and willingly risking negativity and disapproval of others. If they were convinced of the rightness of their views as consistent with the Word of God, they spoke up for something bigger than themselves. Rather than testing the matter as one that was politically correct, the men I followed, while wise and careful, nevertheless stood on biblical, theological, moral, and spiritual principles.

Unashamedly, I was drawn to what many would characterize as "big preachers." Let me explain the concept: "big preachers" were spiritual fathers known as denominational titans, pastors of large congregations, gifted, insightful artisans of preaching, well-known and well-respected by their peers, with a national following (before the Internet, YouTube, Twitter, and television ministries). Among this group I am thankful to God for the global influence of my long-time pastor and spiritual mentor, Dr. Edward V. Hill of Los Angeles. Equally important, God brought me under the sway of a pastor from my undergraduate days and beyond, Dr. Abraham H. Newman of Richmond, California. Then, in graduate studies, I came under the spiritual influence of Dr. Jessie Dawson of Fort Worth, Texas.

Each liberally shared critical wisdom, deep insight, and unusual knowledge regarding God and the advancement of His kingdom. In every way, people and the human condition were of utmost importance to them. With gratitude to these three particularly, I carry that same "people matter" philosophy.

2. **GIFTED COMMUNICATORS OF THE WORD OF GOD, CENTERED IN CHRIST**

Two other spiritual leaders, voices from another era, who greatly influenced me were the late Dr. Manuel L. Scott Sr. of Los Angeles (whom I succeeded in my first pastorate) and then of Dallas; and the late Dr. A. Louis Patterson of Houston. Both taught me the love of the English language, and its power to convey central concepts regarding Christ and the kingdom of God. Not surprisingly, over the years I have taken on similar shadings of speech and delivery, though never fully reaching the level of these masters of Christian leadership and preaching. The maxim holds true that "Imitation is the sincerest form of flattery." I plead guilty to aspiring to preach in an anointed, poetic, scholarly fashion. Words and a Word-centered style with Jesus Christ at its apex capture my approach to Christian proclamation.

Years later, I can still hear Dr. Patterson, with absolute artful articulation built on alliteration: "Christ is all-sufficient for every culture, class, creed, color, circumstance, and condition." Or, I recall Dr. Scott, using language, body, and gesticulations: "As in dominoes, Christian ministers need to learn to play as partners, rather than as cutthroat competitors."

Those simple excerpts from sermonic treasures of the spiritual fathers should assist all clergy in measuring the magnitude of prayerfulness, brilliance, anointing, scholarship, exegesis, and craftsmanship by which I learned what constituted biblical preaching and Christian ministry.

Among African-American Baptists of the last fifty years, these men were in all respects "big preachers." I still praise God for allowing me to observe their ways and their interactions with colleagues and younger clergy as we moved through the hallowed halls of our beloved denomination, the National Baptist Convention. My connections to them opened wonderful doors for Christian service. Additionally, treasured colleagues and opportunities emerged from spiritual fathers who were known as straight shooters; they expressed biblical views and moral positions without fear of being quoted. In fact, they were recognized as "big" precisely because they were unafraid of the negative opinions of the masses.

3. COURAGE OF CONVICTIONS

Instead, these spiritual fathers taught me the high premium attached to one's exhibiting courage to stand on his convictions. While it seems a quaint notion today, amid "trial balloons," polling, consensus, and the like, they were ultimately concerned with "What is right?"

For the minority who might take offense at my use of the big-preacher label for Christian clergy, let me advance the notion that Old Testament scholarship distinguishes major prophets (Isaiah, Ezekiel, Jeremiah) from minor ones (Daniel, Hosea, Joel, Amos, Obadiah, Jonah, Micah, Nahum, Habakkuk, and so forth).

Admittedly, the designation has to do with the comparative length of written prophetic material, along with comparative duration of service to God. In much the same way, contemporary clergy are accorded deference, honor, national recognition, and more by virtue of influence, range of ministry, oratorical gifts, and other humanistic evaluations.

To polish the point, all who are called by God, anointed by Him to declare life-giving truth which culminates in the matchless Son of God, Jesus Christ, through the power of the Holy Spirit, for the advancement of God's kingdom, have merit, significance, standing, and status. Indeed, unlike humanity, God is not a "respecter of persons" (see Acts 10:34). At the same time, our rewards in glory will not be the same. Relative to the quality and quantity of our works, God will ultimately evaluate each of us (cf. 1 Corinthians 3:13ff).

Another aspect of the spiritual fathers under whom God graciously shaped my ministry was their capacity to give me (and everyone) their absolute word. For the three aforementioned father figures, their "yes" was a definite "yes." They did not deal in abstractions, generalizations, or equivocations.

I praise God for their unwillingness to posture, to preen, or to pander to the audience of the moment. In crucial moments when I needed to know where they stood on a particular matter, I could count on a clear word. Practically, this meant that if I followed their directives and trouble ensued, I could always depend on their prayers, support, and love in my time of crisis. That dependence fed my sense of security.

4. SECURITY TO HIS CHILDREN IN THE FAITH

One of the great hallmarks of a spiritual father, in my view, involves his ability to generate security in his progeny. The new way to state this concept is, colloquially, "he has my back." Well, before the formulation, these fathers definitely and definitively always watched my back in Christian ministry.

5. LACK OF VISION FROM GOD IMPERILS CHRISTIAN MINISTRY EFFECTIVENESS

When Christian leaders operate without a clear vision from God (strengthened by exposure to strong, godly, accomplished spiritual fathers), they revert to stale tradition, maintenance ministry, or mimicry of celebrated models, never developing their full identity as Christian leaders.

Vision from God cannot be purchased at some local emporium. Vision from God cannot be found in a compelling book (aside from the Bible!). Vision from God cannot be borrowed from another leader. Vision from God cannot be gleaned from a denominational brochure.

Vision from God cannot be given by an influential national leader. Vision from God cannot be copied from a religious manual. Vision from God cannot be imparted, even, from a loving spiritual father.

Instead, vision from God emanates from time in the prayer chamber, alone with the heavenly Father. In those precious moments, He sensitizes His leaders to the plight of those seated in the pews, in the sanctuary. Through dynamic encounters in the faith realm, God discloses His will for kingdom advancement. When every proposition finds its fulfillment in Christ, we discover vision from God.

6. LEADERS ARE PIVOTAL IN THE KINGDOM OF GOD

In the broad portrait of dynamic Christianity, leaders are central to achieving the task of human redemption. I sincerely believe that God holds those gifted persons (apostles, prophets, evangelists, pastor-teachers) named in the book of Ephesians directly responsible for the "equipping of the saints for the work of service, to the building up of the body of Christ; until we all attain to the unity of the faith, and of the knowledge of the Son of God, to a mature man, to the measure of the stature which belongs to the fullness of Christ" (Ephesians 4:12-13).

The "work of service" establishes that there is more to Christianity than beliefs; we also add to it, behaviors. The work I sense more clergy need to engage in involves reaching the unsaved while teaching and training the saved to serve others in the name of Christ.

7. EXEMPLIFY A "ONE-THING" PROPOSITION

Dr. Billy Graham has for sixty years lived with one consuming passion: that the unsaved throughout the world come to know the Savior. Today, I would encourage young clergy to make that same mission their lodestar.

Let me cite another example of the "one-thing" proposition. I attended a beautiful dinner as the supportive family and dedicated congregation of a dear brother in Christ celebrated his fifty years as a Christian minister. Throughout the dinner, various persons congratulated him on scores of memorable messages. Parishioners spoke of the blessings those messages brought during times of personal crisis, mental stress, bereavement, family calamity, financial ruin, and more.

"Dr. Melvin V. Wade Sr., befitting fifty-plus years of Christian preaching, exemplifies a 'One-thing' brother!" Local politicians sent congratulatory proclamations, acknowledging this milestone in ministry. A hundred colleagues paid tribute to him for his faithfulness to God. Some of us travelled across America to salute him.

As many referred to my friend, they did not speak of his political advocacy (though he did stand for social justice). Nor did they speak of his acclaim to the non-Christian world (though celebrities attended his church). Rather, the dominant focus remained on his consistency in lifting the name of the Savior. Here is what was being celebrated.

Over fifty years under all manner of challenge (personal, seasonal, relational, physical, and spiritual), God had used one man to pray, study, prepare, and deliver perhaps two sermons per Sunday, over fifty-two weeks (that is 104 per year). Then, that number should be multiplied by fifty years (that is approximately 5,200 messages). And as he constantly travels across America as a guest speaker for seminars, lectures, conferences, teaching, and revivals, the number of messages delivered over those fifty years might reach to 8,000!

8. THE COACH MENTALITY AT WORK

Grizzled, tough, legendary football coaches say it often: "Guys, just give it everything you've got, every play, every game, every season. Leave it all [on the field, on the court, at the arena]. That's how we will win." In my imagination, God shares the same sentiment, using spiritual fathers to convey the importance of maintaining a purposeful perspective every day.

In practical terms, fathers in the faith should relish their role in reminding younger Christian leaders that they represent the gracious, loving God of the universe whose love for humanity was on sterling display in sending His Son as the Savior. Those graciously called by God to convey that Christ message should, accordingly, represent the kingdom of God, operating from the highest standards of devotion, character, and love for Him.

9. NEVER SATISFIED, IF ANOTHER CAN DO BETTER!

As with the athletic coach watching every play, every move, keen to his players' strengths and weaknesses, constantly adjusting and adapting to changing circumstances, we need spiritual mentors (fathers in the faith) to gauge the spiritual progress of their young charges.

In the athletic arena, some gifted players resent too much coaching, relishing reliance upon natural athleticism. Those who reach elite status, however, humble themselves to a coach who may or may not have reached stardom in a professional career. For example, in NBA circles neither Phil Jackson nor Pat Riley was a particularly brilliant player; but, each coach has patiently and thoroughly honed champions (Jackson/Michael Jordan; Jackson/Kobe Bryant; Riley/Magic Johnson; Riley/Dwayne Wade).

So I covet those spiritual mentors who will relentlessly push their sons and daughters to fulfill all within them. This task requires conveying that, despite personal satisfaction, a mentor knows there is more potential that remains un-tapped. As an objective observer, the mentor challenges his protégé to more prayer, meditation, reflection, Bible study, reading, and conversations. The whole point involves getting the protégé to dig deeper within, while giving absolute glory to God in the advancement of His kingdom.

As a younger preacher, I hosted a Sunday evening radio program that aired my sermons. In a conversation, my pastor chided me regarding a message he heard. I wanted to hear his analysis. His words were cutting, dissolving my hubris: "As I drove home from worship, I heard your talk the other night." Talk! I was really embarrassed. My little bubble was burst. He did not even have the courtesy of calling it a bad sermon!

In hindsight, as a godly mentor he intended to push me beyond seminary training, great books read, quotes, allusions, analogies, illustrations, and beautiful outlines developed to sharing an encounter with God so that others could experience the presence of God. My feeble study of the Scripture passage, linguistic insight, and subsequent sermon crafting paled in comparison to elevating the Savior, Jesus Christ. After all that, I learned that the power must emanate from heaven if good results are to ensue on the earth.

10. ENSURE SUBSTANTIVE, SUPERNATURAL, SPIRITUAL TRANSMISSION OF TRUTH

With so much fluff, fantastic, and flowery preaching today, Christendom needs substantive, supernatural, spiritual truth which directs absolute deference to Jesus Christ. Preachers must not waste the time of loyal parishioners with theory, imagination, erudition, flights of fancy, needless displays of vocabulary, or intense Hebrew/Greek/Latin lessons, only to miss the Savior!

As I write these words, I am reminded of the gusto of spiritual father figures, taking listeners on a veritable journey of discovery. Thirty or forty years ago, Christ-themed preaching seemed mystical, monumental, marvelous, and miraculous. Something happened as the preached Word went forth: lives and destinies were altered for time and eternity! People were filled with the Holy Spirit, seen in verifiable expressions: tears, running, leaping, dancing, shouts of joy, new resolutions, and changed behaviors, totally repudiating their old lives.

Today, I am afraid many ministers are lauded by congregants for delivering a "good sermon." I simply cannot imagine Old Testament prophets, our Savior, or the disciples receiving favorable reviews for their proclamation. "Thus says the Lord" is not usually accorded magnanimous approval by the masses.

Though I may be unable to fully capture it, when we approach the Word of God, we are moving into the supernatural, the transcendent, and the miraculous. So truly hearing its profound assertions regarding the Creator, His love for humanity, the human predicament (sin), and all God does in sending His Son, Jesus Christ, as the sole agent of reconciliation, takes humanity into another, uniquely distinct dimension of reality.

For that reason, I celebrate spiritual fathers who disallowed trafficking in the trivial as a minister comes before the people of God in a worship experience or a teaching session. Thirty or forty minutes in the pulpit represents a tremendous opportunity for a minister to merge two worlds: the heavenly and the mundane.

Within the parameters of the theme of this book—spiritual mentors matter—I encourage younger clergy to cultivate the perspective of the stalwart warriors of Christendom.

12

THE PARTNERSHIP OF A SPIRITUAL FATHER

A commercial advertisement for an insurance company depicts two families (a young couple and an older one) out for dinner. When the check for the meal arrives, we begin to understand the nature of these relationships. A son reaches for the bill, with his "thought-voice" speaking: *"I'm glad that I prepared for this day."* As the son reaches for the bill, the older gentleman looks at him. The father's "thought-voice" speaks: *"I hope he has enough for this."* The son expresses gratitude for the ability and privilege of paying for the entire meal. In this warm tableau, father and son are inextricably bound in love and respect for the other.

At some point, in the Christian context, a spiritual mentor and his protégé reach beyond the chronological dynamic becoming, over time, trusted, loyal, dependable partners in advancing the kingdom of God. In a word, having been given influence by God among the people of God, leaders should use such to the betterment of the human condition, much more than personal fame and global notoriety.

While reading recently, I came across a riveting booklet by an esteemed gentleman, Dr. Charles Satchell Morris. Its title is arresting: *Noblesse Oblige* (simply stated, noble persons are obligated to serve others).

Spiritual fathers, in my view, should promote among younger clergy several considerations: 1) Maintaining godly reverence; 2) Daring pursuits for God; 3) Powerful prayer and wonderful worship; 4) Reliance upon the inspired, inerrant, infallible, authoritative Word of God; 5) Affirming the centrality of Christ; 6) Living by the anointing of God's Holy Spirit; 7) Celebration of family and integrity; and 8) Commitment to reaching the lost. All of these functions occur in the name of Christ, advancing God's kingdom.

Let's consider the following partnership precepts, transmitted by spiritual fathers:

1. MAINTAINING GODLY REVERENCE

Perhaps today in the Christian church's rush to accommodate its culture, too many young leaders have jettisoned the reverent in a rush toward what they see as relevant. A few current examples might make the point better: the former chancel/altar is now the stage; the sacred pulpit is now the informal podium; and the blessed congregation is now simply the audience. In my view, we need some spiritual fathers to remind younger clergy of the value of walking in established ways, even as we eagerly embrace twenty-first-century methodologies.

Indeed, I am not simply arguing against nomenclature. Instead, the motivations for new terminology dilute the message of biblical adherence. In a word, more of us in Christendom should employ distinctly biblical terms so as to set ourselves apart from this cynical, secular, hollow world system.

The larger matter involves Christians' following cultural norms, rather than presenting American culture with a contrasting biblical, theological, spiritual, and moral worldview. Christian orthodoxy advocated by veterans of the faith will immeasurably impact the work of God's kingdom in Christ, to the degree that fathers in the faith strongly urge maintenance of godly reverence.

2. DARING PURSUITS FOR GOD

With the divine love principle embedded in my psyche, I have been prompted by godly fathers toward daring pursuits for God's honor, glory, and kingdom expansion. The question I ask is this: "What can I do, fully assured of God's love and grace in Christ?" The answer resounds from Scripture: "I can do all things through Him who strengthens me" (Philippians 4:13).

Moreover, when I reach the point of depletion of my strength, I still celebrate God's love: "For I am convinced that [nothing] . . . will be able to separate us from the love of God, which is in Christ Jesus our Lord" (Romans 8:38a, 39b). Within the immediate Romans 8 context, we see a plethora of challenges (death, life, angels, principalities, things present, things to come, powers, height, depth, or any created thing). Or when I appraise external threats, I am reminded of internal resources: "greater is He who is in you than he who is in the world" (1 John 4:4b).

3. POWERFUL PRAYER AND WONDERFUL WORSHIP

Long ago when the fathers spoke to me regarding prayer, they taught me to pray over against how to pray. In the former, it becomes the believer's first default mechanism amid every challenge. In the latter, prayer is a rote mechanism, invoking certain words and phrases with fervor.

A powerful image in my memory bank involves praying with a spiritual mentor during a time of challenge when the odds were genuinely not in my favor! I vividly recall a spiritual father shifting me into the arms of the heavenly Father for assurance, comfort, and guidance. I went from one father to the infinite Father!

Call it the "organized church," "institutional church," "high church," "little church house," or whatever—if saints are there in the name of God with Christ affirmed, I feel at home! Years ago, Pastor Shirley Ceasar said it right: "Hold my mule; I'll shout right here!"

4.   RELIANCE UPON THE INSPIRED, INERRANT, INFALLIBLE, AND AUTHORITATIVE WORD OF GOD

The Southern Baptist Convention, our white brothers and sisters in the Christian faith, have never deviated from a firm position on the accuracy and durability of the Word of God. Their "great ministers" (the late Dr. W. A. Criswell, the late Dr. Adrian Rogers, Bailey Smith, Charles Stanley, Ed Young, Jack Graham, and others) and seminary professors (Al Mohler, Paige Patterson, Roy Fish, Harper Shannon, and others) were adamant regarding the well-established foundation of Scripture. These father figures knew that Christian orthodoxy rested on Scripture. In a world of crumbling foundations, they affirmed the supremacy of God's revelation of Himself culminating in Jesus Christ, the Word made flesh.

5.   AFFIRMING THE CENTRALITY OF CHRIST

Caring spiritual patrons who talked incessantly of the centrality of Christ—for access to God, ongoing faith, eternal life, having prayers granted, and, truly, the entirety of the Christian life—are special gifts from God.

6.   LIVING BY THE ANOINTING OF GOD'S HOLY SPIRIT

As a Baptist, I affirm the union of saints in that my Pentecostal and charismatic family, male and female, should be welcomed to our church family as we find common ground with them. Note the Scripture's exhortation: "There is neither Jew nor Greek, there is neither slave nor free man, there is neither male nor female; for you are all one in Christ Jesus" (Galatians 3:28). Indeed, there is one heaven for all the redeemed in Christ!

In my view, younger clergy must totally rely upon God's Holy Spirit. We need Him much more than gimmicks, charisma, wit, erudition, scheming, or any other human ploy. Those things capture attention for a moment; but then, people will expect another "cute" emphasis. Yet, when God's Spirit prevails, He brings the missing dynamic to everything connected with the kingdom of God. Today, more saints of God need to function in the overflow of the supernatural.

7. CELEBRATION OF FAMILY AND INTEGRITY

We should be proud of the fact that, led by Christian leaders, the family has always been a sacred institution in the black context. Historically, slave owners sought to break the spirits of blacks, diminishing their desires for freedom by disrupting or even failing to acknowledge black families. Yet, they could not shake what God ordained!

8. COMMITMENT TO REACHING THE LOST

In the final reckoning, partnerships develop between older and younger clergy as they share sublime truth.

Technology has been noteworthy as new methods (like research done on iPads, or looking up Scripture on iPhones) have been adopted by old-school godly fathers! The dynamic between spiritual fathers' wisdom and spiritual sons' technological savvy, for example, represents a great model for Christian engagement. Mentors enjoy the spirited back-and-forth achieved when their ideas, expertise, and exposure are celebrated, while opening themselves to contemporary jargon, notions, and trends as long as they respect foundations of biblical, spiritual, relational, cultural, and practical truth, all centering in Jesus Christ. On the other hand, insightful protégés should enjoy the anecdotes, reflections, and gravitas of fathers, taking advantage of hard-earned insight without all the heartaches. A mentor exposes a protégé to the mentor's body of knowledge so that the protégé can bypass the pain of the process.

Therefore, spiritual fathers motivate succeeding generations of saints by their unbridled zeal for God, for His glory, and for taking new territory in the faith dimension.

Indeed, I am deeply moved when an elder statesman of the Christian pulpit says, "Collier, I have been thinking about . . . ."

It signals to me that the Caleb spirit is alive and well in him. Endowed wisdom yearns for places to share it, for the benefit of the next generation of Christian leaders and congregants.

Now, a father may have informed me as to his thoughts so as to engage me in the implementation of those plans. If so, I am ready for the "fight," if aided by his wise counsel. That is what I envision and what underpins this book: spiritual fathers and spiritual sons yoked in battle, leading the forces of Christ, advancing the kingdom of God.

When it is right and affirming, nothing surpasses the wonder of a dynamic mentor-and-protégé relationship in Christ. I know, because I have seen and experienced one, with results still coming forth!

My two spiritual fathers (about whom the full story deserves another book on grace, timing, and circumstances) taught me the value of priority in reaching the lost. Dr. Edward V. Hill and Dr. Abraham H. Newman worked tirelessly to embed that simple yet transcendent concept in my heart: God's mission for the church of the Lord Jesus remains that of sharing the love of God through Christ with all of humanity. Ultimately, they insisted, people matter to God as they are endowed with His image, are made in His likeness, possess infinite worth and dignity, and are deserving of eternal life with the heavenly Father in glory, through Christ's potent sacrifice on Calvary.

Though both men went to be with the Lord in 2003, I am to this day inspired by their insistence upon the foundational concept of reaching the lost. They would not relent from that evangelistic pursuit. They explored new ways of conveying that awesome love from God to unsaved millions. Unapologetically, they tirelessly championed Christ's mandate to every believer. They longed for new methods to creatively deploy the Christian masses to the evangelistic field for optimal impact in reaching the lost.

Today, moved by God's Word, the urgency of salvation, and the clear mandate of Christ, I am motivated by these fathers in particular to teach, preach, and, hopefully, live out that soul-winning notion. In effect, then, my mentors and I became partners in passionate pursuit of the unsaved in our midst. In the best formulation, I trust that we developed a spiritual kinship, rising to the likes of Paul and Timothy.

Moreover, I fondly recall our partnership in another way. Both fathers referenced above, before they were called from labor to rest in the arms of the heavenly Father, invited me to lead revivals at their respective churches. Talk about nervous! I wanted each to respect that I was serious regarding souls. I can only speculate that the preaching theme I chose—sharing the Christian faith with the lost—made for a long three days of preaching! In that period, with my continuing maturity in Christ, we discussed Christian ministry, not in the terms of how many attended worship; nor how much by way of finances were generated; nor the state of our facility; nor the influence of congregants. Instead, they keenly inquired as to new souls, frequency of baptisms, restorations to faithfulness, ministries, or eternal impact for the kingdom of God.

13

THE PRINCIPLES OF A SPIRITUAL FATHER

The notion of the important role played by spiritual fathers must be viewed through the prism of the innumerable principles and enduring lessons they convey to their children. Principles represent a general rule or truth on which others are based, or they are a fundamental doctrine or belief. In my judgment, they are foundational for a well-ordered life. In a world too often given to celebration of the transitory, it is refreshing to view persons living according to principles, especially when they derive from the Word of God. Those charged by God with the heavy responsibility for the propagation of principles from the spiritual realm are the fathers in the faith.

Wittingly or not, fathers are adept at sharing godly insight with younger clergy. Daily, God wonderfully uses godly fathers to "speak into" the lives of those who affirm them as spiritual mentors. Small matters take on additional substance when anointed fathers explain the deeper significance of what is being discussed. The following are a few example principles upon which my Christian leadership paradigm has been constructed, with assistance from spiritual fathers.

1. PASTORAL LEADERSHIP

In 1983, as a newly minted pastor, I was excited by the prospect of hosting my undergraduate pastor and spiritual father as one of my first guest speakers. As I knew he would, he did a masterful job in the message. He reminded us of our evangelistic responsibility (sharing our faith in Christ with all humanity, seeking to lead them to a personal life commitment). As was customary, we would give any guest speaker an "honorarium" (love token for his message). I asked our church financial secretary/treasurer, a fine man, to prepare the check; and to present it to my pastor. The secretary did as I instructed. I thought I had conducted myself well in this important pastoral responsibility.

My spiritual father, on the other hand, called me into my own office, set me down, and gave me an important lesson in pastoral leadership: I should always hand any guest the check in an envelope! Now, many people reading that admonition might wonder as to the principle; or, ask, why is it so significant? I learned that day, and have practiced over thirty years since, exactly what he told me. Here is the point: a Christian leader is ultimately accountable to God, to the people of that congregation, and to himself. As such, he must know and take responsibility for the actions of that congregation, in all respects. Of course, the leader cannot achieve or undertake all things alone. Yet, he must not plead ignorance regarding critical matters, such as church finances. In this instance, the guest speaker should view himself as the guest of the pastor, speaking to the congregation.

In my experience, in more than three decades of speaking in various congregations across America, I am there, primarily, because of the invitation of that pastoral leader. I sit where he designates. I literally move at his behest. I aim to be in sync with his leadership model. While I am to honor God with a message from the Word of God, I really want my host to sense an anointed message from heaven, centering in Jesus Christ, aiming to draw saints of God closer to Him for the advancement of His kingdom. After I leave there, I trust that people will feel a connection with God, giving appreciation to that pastoral leader for allowing me to visit. By such a good "day" of worship and preaching, all are happy!

All of the above distilled down to a simple pastoral principle: everything in the church begins with a conscientious leader. Leaders must never view their roles as peripheral, secondary, or trivial. They should, then, live with the sense that they will be held responsible: "Remember those who led you, who spoke the word of God to you; and considering the result of their conduct, imitate their faith" (Hebrews 13:7); or, "Obey your leaders and submit to them, for they keep watch over your souls as those who will give an account. Let them do this with joy and not with grief, for this would be unprofitable for you" (Hebrews 13:17). People elected, affirmed, or followed the Christian leader for a reason. When leaders of any stripe express ignorance as to what occurs in their domain of service, they should long recall President Harry S. Truman's dictum: "The buck stops with me."

2. PUBLICLY EXPRESS APPRECIATION TO COLLEAGUES

I have inculcated another profound principle from a father in the faith. The late Dr. Manuel Scott Sr., whom I followed in my first pastorate at the age of 22 in Los Angeles, taught me (and legions of others) an invaluable lesson: Prior to starting a preaching moment as guest speaker "in another man's pulpit," take a brief moment to publicly express appreciation to that Christian leader! It is, in my view, unconscionable to begin speaking as a visiting minister without remembering who facilitated the invitation in the first place. These few words also serve to "warm up" the audience, thus enhancing the preaching experience. It further builds pastor-pastor rapport, with congregants hearing gratitude from the speaker, which is very important in a day of self-preening speakers. There should be a genuine appreciation for one who serves God and His people by one of his colleagues. If those of us in Christian ministry do not honor our fellows, will anyone else do it? I think not!

In the larger sense, these initial principles offered by experienced fathers were aimed at building lifelong ties necessary for a successful Christian ministry. In both cases, nothing in my undergraduate studies, or my graduate seminary studies for that matter, had prepared me for the intricacies of leadership dynamics at the congregational level. Allow me to mount a soap-box here: many of my colleagues are "spiritual orphans" (lacking a spiritual father figure in their lives). Accordingly, they make many fatal errors as pastoral leaders because they did not receive, nor have they sought, hands-on instruction from clergy elders in connecting with parishioners at the personal level. In my experience, people tend to follow principled leadership that is visionary, direct, clear, loving, and intentional, within a matrix of established advancement of God's kingdom through the Lord, Jesus Christ.

3.   TRUE HUMILITY BEFORE GOD

Moreover, from sainted fathers, I saw the principle of true humility before God. I respect those fathers who understood their lives as being specifically sanctioned by divine favor. The Scriptures validated the concept: "He has told you, O man, what is good; And what does the LORD require of you But to do justice, to love kindness, And to walk humbly with your God?" (Micah 6:8); or, "Whoever exalts himself shall be humbled; and whoever humbles himself shall be exalted" (Matthew 23:12); or, "Therefore humble yourselves under the mighty hand of God, that He may exalt you at the proper time" (1 Peter 5:6).

My mentors found it objectionable and offensive if one made too much reference to self, without honoring God in heaven. Looking back, I now appreciate a father who, hearing me make an intemperate statement, lovingly corrected me: "Perhaps you meant to say that God used you in that recent endeavor . . ." Rightly, he cautioned against my sophomoric proclivities in a preponderance of personal pronouns ("I, I, I"). From then until now, I have consciously tried to control, through humility before God, any sense that I can achieve anything in the spiritual realm without the power and grace of God. The Bible clarified it: "apart from Me you can do nothing" (John 15:5b). Indeed, all the glory for any achievement must flow back to God!

4. RESPECT THE CHRISTIAN FAITH TRADITION

In candor, at several junctures along my pastoral pilgrimage, probably because I have been considerably younger than the governing structure of tradition-bound congregations, I have needed healthy doses of sage, practical fatherly advice. I have needed to blend "Behold, I will do something new" (Isaiah 43:19a) with the great hymn "Faith of Our Fathers." Only through the power of God can one be both traditional and creative. Curbing my youthful zeal, the overriding lesson the fathers in the faith sought to convey was a simple one: "Son, try to understand the perspective of others. Try to meet and manage the fears of those in the pews."

My response has always been this: "As a thankful Baptist, I yearn to celebrate the full dimensions of God's kingdom intention. I pray to bring 'traditionalists' along the journey of embracing new ways of extending God's love through Christ to all humanity." In this regard, I am trapped by a troubling verse from Scripture: "Nor do people put new wine into old wineskins; otherwise the wineskins burst, and the wine pours out and the wineskins are ruined; but they put new wine into fresh wineskins, and both are preserved" (Matthew 9:17). Old Christian institutions need new vitality, new thinking, new methods, new systems, and new perspectives. Yet, a case can be made for respect for the biblically sound traditions. At this point, only the Holy Spirit in His miraculous manifestation can handle the old "wineskins," giving them vitality and elasticity for the contemporary Christian witness. Therefore, this principle yet unfolds for me.

Without destroying an enduring Christian institution built on Christ, they helped me to become a better Christian leader. Clearly, the enemy of God's cause would provoke Christian leaders and congregations to engage in petty arguments, in the process forsaking the larger agenda of kingdom expansion through Christ. Fundamentally, all who helped to shape my leadership philosophy were in unanimity on one principle: Be prepared to fight for a biblical principle. Absolute loyalty to the inerrant, inspired authoritative Word of God was a must! Jesus Christ as the sole means of reconciliation before God was sacrosanct. The present indwelling and effective work of the Holy Spirit was critical for the life of the church. A praying congregation was a non-negotiable. A soul-winning one, also, was beyond debate. A holy people for God was worth standing up for. Supporting the mission of the church through tithes and offerings was at the core of biblical stewardship. Along with a few more significant doctrines, Christian leaders must discern what is vital, over against what may be a pet peeve of a particular leader.

5. GUARD THE TREASURE OF CHRIST

I say this with complete respect and reverence to the fathers (departed and those still alive): In the main, they were not enamored or impressed by lofty theories, esteemed theologians, trendy concepts, or brash book titles. Yet, the ones who guided me were resolute in affirming core principles that had been handed down to them by their spiritual fathers. The fathers I followed gave voice to a timeless principle: Christian clergy live with a great treasure. The Scripture affirmed it: "Guard, through the Holy Spirit who dwells in us, the treasure which has been entrusted to you" (2 Timothy 1:14); or, "The things which you have heard from me in the presence of many witnesses, entrust these to faithful men who will be able to teach others also" (2 Timothy 2:2).

From Christ to the apostle Paul to Timothy to my fathers in the faith, all the way down to me, I recognize an unbroken chain of responsibility for safe-guarding the Christian "jewels." This "treasure" of the Christian Gospel, however, resides in flawed, broken, pitiful "earthen vessels" (2 Corinthians 4:7). If I do my part to ensure that the next generation receives the message, intact, as I previously received it, I will feel that my ministry for Christ has been successful, to the glory of God. In a real sense, propagation of the Christian way is done by intentional instilling of a body of truth centering in Christ for each successive generation.

6. FATHERS TRANSMIT SPIRITUAL VALUES

Called by God as fathers in the faith, blessed by their progeny, such fathers must cultivate a cultural affinity for a set of ideals, values, and sincerity regarding all that constitutes the Christian notion of the expansion of Christ's kingdom. The principle is sound: fathers transmit biblical, moral, theological, spiritual, practical perspectives to younger clergy, helping the latter to reject isms and ideologies which are antagonistic and antithetical to the Christian worldview. When they are successful, Christian clergy in the twenty-first century will be enhanced, with their congregations immeasurably impacted, as they exemplify Christ, and draw others to the kingdom.

7. PUNCTUALITY

A seminal principle I took from a colossal figure, functioning as a spiritual father in my life, was punctuality. Dr. Abraham H. Newman of Richmond, California, my undergraduate pastor, was a stickler for time. If the church bulletin (what he called the "worksheet") read the start of the gathering as 10:45 a.m., Dr. Newman was really ready to begin at 10:30 a.m. And he had a definite timeframe for the conclusion of the worship. For him, time in God's work involved a moral imperative: "Break up your fallow ground, For it is time to seek the LORD" (Hosea 10:12b); or, "There is an appointed time for everything" (Ecclesiastes 3:1a); or, "Let us not lose heart in doing good, for in due time we will reap if we do not grow weary" (Galatians 6:9).

With all my heart, throughout my ministry for Christ, I have yearned to be respectful of time. The guiding idea communicated was this: How people treat time reflects itself in other areas of their lives. Indeed, discipline in time management underscores discipline in other facets of existence: prayerfulness, Bible study, regular giving to God's kingdom, general spending, turning in assignments, or keeping one's word. If I have been late, it was not the fault of Dr. Newman. Rather, I got a late start, and then tried to make up for it ("Lord, please forgive my excessive speed on the freeways.")

Additionally, I applaud Dr. Newman (and other fathers in my life) for modeling intentional morality before God. "Doc" was married to his first wife for well more than fifty-five years; she died in Atlanta, while attending the National Baptist Convention session. (I was in the room with him and a few others. The pain of his loss was palpable.) True to his biblical, moral, ethical compass, after a few years, he remarried a Christian woman, thus setting another godly example. I, therefore, salute this spiritual father for the wisdom, gravity, and substance he displayed as I observed him over the course of forty years.

Under his care, tutelage, and influence, God forged me on an anvil of faithfulness. In that time, interestingly, we never discussed sports, television drama, or gossip, or engaged in frivolity. Yes, we did laugh, but it was a brief departure from the norm. This was a man of rectitude and reverence for God, symbolized in the trajectory of his life and ministry. Throughout a distinguished Christian ministry, he projected an assertive, bold, visionary image of leadership. While in his presence, persons were quite careful in their speech, for it might occasion an impromptu teaching seminar. "Doc" was also passionate regarding evangelism (sharing Christ as Savior with all humanity). There is no doubt in my mind as to the source of my similar sense of the bedrock principle of evangelism for the Christian witness today.

Late in his life, Dr. Newman invited me to preach a revival at his church. After forty-plus years there, I am proud to say, he was still envisioning ways to enhance that congregation. At a time when most had their "landing gear" down, here was a man still excited about new converts, new plans, and new ways of outreach to humanity. Until his transition to glory in 2003, he possessed the Caleb spirit of godly leadership: "Now behold, the LORD has let me live . . . and now behold, I am eighty-five years old today. I am still as strong today as I was in the day Moses sent me; . . . Now then, give me this hill country . . ." (Joshua 14:10-11, 12a). At least monthly, the Spirit of God brings back to my memory some great "pearl" of wisdom from this generous, dignified, compassionate father in the faith. Today, I am richer for his many deposits in my life. And, the people whom I serve are recipients of a vast treasure of godly information.

8.   READ WISELY AND THINK DEEPLY

In so many ways, I am profoundly grateful to spiritual fathers for passing on the principle of reading wisely and thinking deeply. At points along my journey, I have been humbled by favorable comparisons to sui generis thinker, mentor, brother, friend, long-time comrade, Dr. A. Louis Patterson of Houston. By common acclaim, "Patt" has given the body of Christ over the last fifty years alliteration as a dynamic aspect of persuasive, creative sermon preparation. In truth, I heard "Patt" as a young Christian, talked with him incessantly after God's call to spiritual service, and heeded his counsel, all while attempting to craft biblical messages in that manner. Throughout thirty years, by God's grace, we have preached with and for one another. To "Patt" I am eternally grateful. What I have sensed in hearing him deliver hundreds of messages over the years was a unique, analytical skill in viewing the Scripture. Then, he applied the alliterative principles to everyday life. Clearly, no one does it as well as the master!

9.   RESPECT SCRIPTURE, HONOR CHRIST

Perhaps the greatest principles I derived from spiritual father figures such as "Patt" and others were these: 1) Have deep respect for the Scripture text; and 2) Always center all preaching in Christ. From "Patt," that latter principle would come out as "The magnificent, majestic, marvelous, miraculous work of the Lord Jesus Christ" (that is an example of alliteration). Seminary professors and other influential authors might refer to such critical emphases as the foundation for persuasive "expository preaching." When the Word becomes the foundation, and Christ the objective, we are well on the way to principles for meaningful lives. Biblical, anointed, effective preaching always builds to a crescendo: what God achieved for humanity culminates in the cross of Calvary, on which Christ was crucified! In a day replete with "life coaches" and "motivational speakers" masquerading in Christian pulpits, we need, instead, Bible-based, Christ-exalting, Spirit-saturated, devil-chasing, moral, creative, dynamic, direct, celebrative preaching. The fathers called such—"flat-footed" preaching—good preaching! I pray that God will use me in such service to His kingdom.

10. YEARN FOR THE SPIRIT'S ANOINTING

At the same time, my beloved pastor, Dr. Edward V. Hill of Los Angeles, was a man of letters and rhetoric, when he put his mind to it. If he felt the occasion warranted it, he could scale the heights of literary taste. In that regard, he quoted Abraham Lincoln: "Better to remain silent and thought a fool, than to speak and remove all doubt." Or, in sermons or conversations, he might add allusions to Kipling's immortal poem "If." Hidden under layers of homespun philosophy, country ways, "Doc" possessed a fertile mind, forever questioning, always pushing sons in the ministry to pursue quality seminary training. Many of us laugh as we reminisce on how he promised "three points," which turned into, "and the fourth thing . . ." There was an unusual anointing from God on him. "Doc" could utter some tough, controversial ideas, and people would acknowledge them—as God gave him insight, humor, charisma, and extreme likeability by the masses. He was at home among diverse audiences—denominationally, ethnically, and geographically. Those who heard him join me in proclaiming, "What a preacher!" The best principle he illustrated was anointing from the Spirit of God. After hearing him, you recognized the truth: "[T]hey were amazed, and began to recognize [him] as having been with Jesus" (Acts 4:13b). Every saint of God, and especially every Christian minister, should aspire to that encomium.

11. ABSOLUTE DEDICATION TO JESUS CHRIST

As I reflect on this man of God, I have been tempted to write a book solely based on the innumerable godly principles that Dr. Hill taught me. I will mention in this space only a small number of them. The first one was absolute dedication to the Lord, Jesus Christ. In every possible way, "Doc" made it clear that Jesus made all the difference for him. He was unequivocal in declaring Jesus as "the way, and the truth, and the life; no one comes to the Father but through Me" (John 14:6). Once, he preached at a seminary before an esteemed audience of theologians, with the simple subject of "What My Momma Told Me about Jesus." In the message, Dr. Hill referenced Christ's virgin birth, His incarnation, His teachings, His miracles, His vicarious death, His bodily resurrection, and His anticipated rapture of the saints. When he finished the message, a professor remarked, "I'd give Dr. Hill's momma an 'A+' in Systematic Theology."

Truly, the fulcrum of this man's life was what God did in dispatching His grace in Christ to a little village in south Texas, saving a poor boy. That manifestation of grace in Christ changed his life trajectory, taking him to cities around the world, to the White House, and beyond. And, in a robust, exciting life, he explained the "secret" of his sacred success: it was all from Jesus Christ!

12. LOVE FOR PEOPLE

Further, this spiritual father loved people—unequivocally, without respect to status or situation. In fact, he was unalterably on the side of the "underdog." Tell him a sad story, and he would try to help. Seeing him help people, some of whose sincerity I doubted, I vowed that I would not follow this principle. Yet, I must confess this: I have found myself helping people in the same ways he did—through financial blessings, dubious stories, aiming to see the best in another, defending people, and expecting more from them.

Moreover, this people principle led "Doc" to embrace various cultures, ethnicities, Christian groups, and, most controversially, conservative, "right-wing" Republicans. Fundamentally, Dr. Hill was a "Jesus preacher." As a herald of Christ, he was comfortable among Presbyterians, Lutherans, Pentecostals, Methodists, Church of God, Fundamentalists, Assembly of God, Independents, Word of Faith, Apostolic, Evangelicals, and any other strand of the Christian family.

Once, I watched in Dallas, Texas, as thousands of white Christians in unison proclaimed him as their great leader. He had just articulated a position they affirmed. Later, when I queried him as to the oddity of this ethnic embrace, he explained that, contrary to popular belief, ethnicities in America have more in common than they even know. Indeed, he taught me this: Remain secure in your identity; stand on the Word; tell the truth—and everything will work out fine. Those nuggets of wisdom have served me well in more than fifty-five years of life, thirty-eight years of Christian ministry, and more than thirty-three years as a Christian minister (pastor, author, lecturer, denominational leader, and activist).

(As much as I respect him, and all he taught me, however, I never embraced my pastor's political perspective. In my view, the current brand of Republicanism is mean-spirited and cold, prone to cutting benefits for vulnerable people under the guise of "austerity" and debt reduction. Also, this new obstructionism will not consider anything President Obama advances, no matter the merits of the proposal. Current Republicanism, moreover, lacks racial diversity. In many ways, such a political party smacks of racism. On the other hand, I am not a pawn in the pocket of Democrats, as they lack moral principles. Electorally, they also take blacks for granted. Therefore, I am a proud Independent. Thus, I advise parishioners to vote principles over party or personality. Affirm that which honors God, Jesus Christ, the Bible, morality, and the poor among us.)

13. REMAIN TRUE TO CORE CONVICTIONS

Another principle that Dr. Hill, my spiritual father, shared with me was for one to remain true to his or her core convictions: "For to me, to live is Christ and to die is gain" (Philippians 1:21); or, "For I determined to know nothing among you except Jesus Christ, and Him crucified" (1 Corinthians 2:2). Many of us close to him remember that if he was convinced of his position, no matter what you said, he would maintain his course. And, if you were not careful, he would persuade you toward his side. "Pastor" was a born debater, advocate, and indefatigable champion for a particular course. Perhaps it was his initial desire to pursue a legal career. And, he would use such linguistic skills to help others. I can attest to this: if he was on your side, he would think of new ways to present your cause in the best light.

14. CAREFULLY EVALUATE EVERY MATTER

In a major way, he fostered respect for the principle of pursuing God's insight above all—as nothing was as simple as it was presented. He always taught that there was more to the issue than was evident at first glance. That principle was vital to me. A bit of healthy skepticism goes a long way. In my view, too many Christian leaders fail because they are, too often, gullible, overly trusting, and, thus, prone to error. I trust the Word: "Behold, I send you out as sheep in the midst of wolves; so be shrewd as serpents and innocent as doves" (Matthew 10:16).

15. DESPITE ALL, MAINTAIN FAITH IN GOD

Equally important is the fact that other spiritual mentors explained, lived, modeled, and reinforced the principle of faith in God. It was not so much an intellectual faith, as it was the kind of faith that meets every challenge, fully assured of God's capacity to channel, change, control, or conquer whatever it is. The Bible is clear on what constitutes faith: "Now faith is the assurance of things hoped for, the convictions of things not seen" (Hebrews 11:1). Such faith is God-centered, Christ-affirming, real, dynamic, and thus deeper than the silliness of positive thinking, psycho-babble, twelve steps, or something heard on television talk shows. In the midst of trying times, the spiritual fathers exemplified what faith in God could achieve: children rescued from addictive lives, homes paid off before time, congregants blessed beyond comprehension, the healing virtue of God, the provisional capabilities of God, God's intervention in a crisis, and so much more.

While many speak of faith as an intellectual exercise, I know it at a deeper level. From the fathers, I learned it as absolute necessity in a well-ordered life: "And without faith it is impossible to please Him, for he who comes to God must believe that He is and that He is a rewarder of those who seek Him" (Hebrews 11:6). The faith notion was such a compelling one that I was inspired by God to write a book on the subject: *Living in the Faith Dimension* (Walker Publishing, 2012).

16. ALWAYS OPERATE IN INTEGRITY

Perhaps the final principle that was given to me by spiritual fathers was a simple yet profound one: Be a man of your word. That is, operate in integrity. Again, the principle was eminently biblical: "But let your statement be, 'Yes, yes' or 'No, no'; anything beyond these is of evil" (Matthew 5:37). At the same time, that one verse, from the perspective of the fathers in the faith, was also eminently practical, in that they felt that if one says that he or she will do a particular thing, then let it be only death (or a near equivalence) that prevents him or her from achieving it. That simple approach to personal integrity would go a distance in strengthening the Christian witness, as Christian leaders would become men and women of their word. I know that is a quaint, almost naïve notion; yet, it is one that I hold dear. In a world of falsehoods, evasions, and "drama," is it too much to ask that God's church (God's preachers, especially) carry themselves as distinct from such cynicism? I would like to answer my own rhetorical question: My fathers in Christ felt that integrity matters!

The cumulative "takeaway" from my exploration of the principles shared by my spiritual fathers, who have shaped my own thinking and philosophy of Christian ministry, is very similar to what occurs in large-scale economics, especially after an investment. Economists speak of "ROI," or "return on investment." I aspire to serve God, His people, and humanity because I am quite mindful of the many "investments" made by men who wanted me to fulfill my personal and spiritual potential. These fathers operated from critical biblical principle: "From everyone who has been given much, much will be required" (Luke 12:48).

While I reflect on my life—now at middle age—I am grateful to God for placing me in these spiritual relationships. I am convinced that God, graciously and providentially, used them as critical guides along my journey of faith. They pushed me toward a good education, gently chided me when I chose less than my best, and loved me in the midst of personal crises. In every case, I sense acutely that each father was carefully watching his emotional, financial, and spiritual investment in my life. At points of a degree of success—growth in Christ, university graduation, seminary completion, initial pastorate, marriage, birth of children, author of several books, national speaking schedule, multiple ministry achievements, activism, and more—I only pray these realities indicate that the "investment" in me was a good one, with "dividends" aplenty.

While the Word may strike some as strange, coming from a Christian minister, ministers are engaged in a noble undertaking; they are, in every sense, professionals. Truly, professional standing really matters to me. Like a medical doctor, attorney, judge, corporate CEO, U.S. Senator, business leader, school superintendent, architect, or related professional, ministry to me represents a unique calling from God. Thus, I value its importance, and I work assiduously to ensure it receives similar consideration by others. Indeed, the professionals listed earlier are the peers of an experienced, prepared, successful minister.

Amid the assaults of the enemy, only the grace of God has kept me from major ministry scandal. Watching others, saddened by the collateral damage to families, ministries, and the kingdom of God, I have tried to avoid a similar outcome. Perhaps what has kept me thus far is that I have never wanted to reflect poorly on God, my commitment to Christ, family, mentors, biblical knowledge, or the people God has given to my spiritual care. That sense of accountability and responsibility holds me steady, while navigating the swift currents of twenty-first-century life. Wisely, I ask prayer from and patience by all, as I consider my life an incomplete symphony, a veritable "work in progress."

If some egregious error were to befall me, bringing shame to the body of Christ in years to come, the fault will definitely not rest upon nonexistent role models. Instead, it would result from succumbing to the allures of the enemy, and my inability to adhere to sound principles conveyed by pious, devout, dedicated, godly fathers. With such a stupendous spiritual deposit, I pray for grace to keep me.

CONCLUSION

In light of these important considerations of a spiritual mentor, we conclude that such seminal figures must epitomize invaluable spiritual traits. Not surprisingly, the best traits of a spiritual father are already revealed in the Word of God. Biblical principles form the basis of practicality. We discover the best fatherly traits in alignment with Galatians 5:22-23: "But the fruit of the Spirit is love, joy, peace, patience, kindness, goodness, faithfulness, gentleness, self-control; against such things there is no law."

Indeed, this agricultural metaphor of fruit is rich with significance. When the seed of God's Holy Spirit is planted in the soil of lives transformed by regeneration through Christ, the resultant harvest of the Spirit's indwelling will be an assortment of fruit. (That's a preach-able outline!)

These nine spiritual varieties/traits are not exhaustive but rather representative of the various traits that are apparent in those daily and continually yielding to God's Holy Spirit. Accordingly, in the best scenario, Christians celebrate spiritual fathers because they embody the following traits:

Love—God's love (Greek: *agape*), irrespective of its object, without necessity of reciprocity, nor evaluation of merit.

Joy—deep, abiding, optimistic, compelling sensation toward all of life, as uniquely, paradoxically, and ultimately ordained by God.

Peace—calm assurance of God's victory, and our best outcome, no matter the temptations, terrors, trials, tests, and taunts we face.

Patience—burnished, honed, molded in the crucible of divine love, ensuring viability for long-term focus, usefulness, and endurance.

Kindness—tender concern in Christ in contrast to a cold, cynical, callous, corrupt culture or worldview.

Goodness—intrinsic consideration of morality, ethics, integrity, truth, transparency, and accountability in all dealings.

Faithfulness—remaining resolute to godly principles, fostering a life of practicality, productivity, and progress in God.

Gentleness—God's grace gift, refuting negativity, cynicism, ugliness, and toxicity.

Self-control—absolute discipline of the human spirit by the Holy Spirit.

Consider that each trait in the spiritual father will, most often, be contrasted in its absence in the protégé. Yet, by God's grace, worship, prayerfulness, study of the Word, obedience, hurt, suffering, observation, analysis, and determination over time through varied experiences, younger clergy will learn time-honored lessons for a full life of dedication to God, while advancing His kingdom through Jesus Christ.

Rev. Dr. Jarvis L. Collier

The Rev. Dr. Jarvis L. Collier serves God, the church, and the community as a twenty-first-century anointed, scholarly, insightful champion of the kingdom, as expressed by the Lord Jesus Christ. His ministry is fresh, alive, dynamic, and results oriented, for the empowerment of saints for relevant engagement.

He is pastor of Pleasant Green Baptist Church in Kansas City, Kansas—a vibrant, growing, historic fellowship with evangelistic, prayer, discipleship, media, private school, 43-unit senior facility, and many other aspects of transformative community impact.

Passionately, he champions a social justice agenda: education; employment, blood donors; skills enhancement; health-care initiatives; wealth generation; parolee reintegration; he is a former Board Chair, United Way, and has plans for urban supermarket, among many community works.

Collier, a native of Los Angeles, came to Christ as a child in 1968. The product of the LA Unified School District, he excelled academically. He possesses a sharp mind, dedicated heart, and strong will. His formal preparation and theological grounding, for the practical dimensions of Christian ministry, include distinguished graduate of the University of California, Los Angeles (UCLA); Fuller Theological Seminary; additional graduate studies at Southwestern Baptist Theological Seminary; and an honorary doctorate.

An active youth, he served in many Baptist capacities from a young age. He was mentored by several giants of Christian ministry who are now resting in glory. He was called by God to full-time Christian ministry in 1978. He has now served God and His church for nearly thirty-five years.

He is the acclaimed author of several books: *Biblical Challenges for Christian Singles; The Preacher's Journey; A Passion for Excellence; Seeking the Kingdom;* and *Living in the Faith Dimension,* which are widely used texts across America for nurture, edification, and Christian engagement.

This "Renaissance Man," (a world traveler who enjoys horseback riding, backgammon, and billiards), enjoys family (wife, Jennifer, and two children), in Kansas City, and is an ardent champion for social justice, locally—nationally, and globally.

BIBLIOGRAPHY

The following books and materials were particularly helpful in developing this book.

I embrace the notion of accuracy in presenting facts, places, events, names, titles, associations, and statistics. Especially are references critical in secular and spiritual notations.

Therefore, daily, I closely read and quote from at least four newspapers: *The New York Times, The Wall Street Journal, USA Today,* and *The Kansas City Star.*

I commend all these resources to every reader for greater insight, reflection, and edification.

Batterson, Mark. *All In*. Grand Rapids: Zondervan, 2013.

Bush, George W. *41: A Portrait of My Father*. New York: Crown Publishers, 2014.

Criswell, W. A. *Great Doctrines of the Bible, Volume 2*. Grand Rapids: Zondervan, 1982.

Gire, Ken. *Seeing What Is Sacred*. Nashville: Thomas Nelson, 2006.

Gladwell, Malcolm. *David and Goliath*. New York: Little, Brown & Co., 2013.

Hanby, Mark. *You Have Not Many Fathers*. Shippensburg, PA: Destiny Image, 1996.

Horton, Michael. *Christless Christianity*. Grand Rapids: BakerBooks, 2008.

Keller, Timothy. *King's Cross*. New York: Dutton/Penguin Group, 2011.

Miller, Calvin. *Letters to a Young Pastor*. Colorado Springs, CO: David C. Cook, 2011.

Osteen, Joel. *You Can, You Will*. New York: Hatchette Book Group/Faith Works, 2014.

Piper, John. *Brothers, We Are Not Professionals*. Nashville: B&H Publishing, 2002.

Pritchard, Ray. *The God You Can Trust*. Eugene, OR: Harvest House, 2003.

————. *Stealth Attack*. Chicago: Moody Publishers, 2007.

Rainer, Thom S. *I Am a Church Member*. Nashville: B&H Publishing Group, 2013.

Smith, Robert, Jr. *Doctrine that Dances*. Nashville: B&H Publishing, 2008.

Wade, James C., Jr. *Not Too Early, Not Too Late: Life After Retirement*. Merrillville, IN: Literacy in Motion Publishing, 2014.

Willams, R. A., Jr. *God, Grits and More*. Bloomington, IN: AuthorHouse, 2006.

Yates, George. *Reaching the Summit*. Bellevue, Canada: Essence Publishing, 2012.

CPSIA information can be obtained at www.ICGtesting.com
Printed in the USA
LVOW10s1229250816

501576LV00004BA/8/P

9 780910 683845